Poems of
C. Day Lewis
1925-1972

Poems of C. Day Lewis 1925-1972

Chosen and with an Introduction by Ian Parsons

JONATHAN CAPE

AND

THE HOGARTH PRESS

This collection first published 1977
Reprinted 1977
Jonathan Cape Limited
30 Bedford Square, London WC1
and
The Hogarth Press
40-42 William IV Street, London WC2

British Library Cataloguing in Publication Data
Day Lewis, Cecil
     Poems of C. Day Lewis, 1925-1972.
     Index.
     ISBN 0-224-01294-0
     ISBN 0-7012-0427-3 (Hogarth Press)
     1. Parsons, Ian
     821'.9'12 PR 6007.A95A17
     English poetry

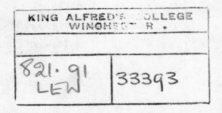
Printed in Great Britain by
Lowe & Brydone Printers Limited, Thetford, Norfolk
and bound by Wm Brendon & Son Ltd, Tiptree, Essex

Contents

Of the Early Poems, *Beechen Vigil* was published by the Fortune Press and *Country Comets* by M. Hopkinson. The next five books were published by The Hogarth Press, and the remainder by Jonathan Cape. Of the translations, those from *The Georgics* and *The Eclogues* were first published by Jonathan Cape, those from *The Aeneid* by The Hogarth Press. The translation of Paul Valéry's *Le Cimetière marin* was first published by Secker & Warburg.

Introduction

One day, perhaps, it will be thought appropriate to bring together in one volume everything Day Lewis wrote; but that day is not yet. It is far too early to attempt to pass judgment on his poetry *sub specie aeternitatis*. What I have done is to choose what seem to me the most typical, the most original, and the most successful in their particular genre, of the very large number of poems (something over 400, excluding translations) that he wrote. In other words, to give contemporary readers the opportunity to assess both the scope and the quality of his poetic gift.

The undertaking presented some difficulties, for Day Lewis was not only a very prolific poet but also an uneven one. He began writing poetry very early, and virtually never stopped — although he tells us in his autobiography that with him 'poetry comes and goes', and that it was in the fallow times that he turned to translation. His fertility had two consequences: one beneficial, the other the reverse. It meant that quite early in his life he came to think of himself as first and foremost a poet, and thereafter he never allowed the exigencies of earning a living, whether as a schoolmaster, a publisher or a writer of detective stories, to deflect him from his total commitment to poetry. But it also meant that he seized eagerly on every opportunity to write a poem — a friend's birthday, sitting for his portrait, or a visit to Ireland (his affection for which, though genuine enough, had an element of self-willed romanticism about it) — regardless of whether the pressure of feeling behind the impulse was sufficient to ensure success. Sometimes it was not. So I have been involved in a winnowing process, an attempt to separate the wheat from the chaff in a very large and varied body of verse.

Day Lewis was nothing if not catholic in his tastes. He

admired a very wide range of poets, and tried his hand at a correspondingly large number of poetic modes: lyric, elegiac, narrative and dramatic. That he was not equally successful in all of them is hardly surprising; what is more surprising is the number of only partially successful poems that he published. But in this he was in very good company. I have always been struck by the number of established English poets who seem to have been unaware of when they were being dull or boring or even downright bad. There is a long line of them, stretching back to Spenser and including Dryden, Wordsworth and Tennyson. Of all modern poets, Hardy most notably exemplified this trait, and it is perhaps not altogether a coincidence that he was a potent influence on Day Lewis. Not that Day Lewis himself was unaware of the uneven quality of his output. As he remarked once to Philip Larkin: 'You write too little — I've written far too much.' And in the Preface to his *Collected Poems 1954* he explained why, unlike Graves and Auden, he had felt unable to disown or revise early work.

'Some poets can rewrite and improve their early work, years later. I wish I could do so: but the selves who wrote those poems are strangers to me, and I cannot resume their identities or go back into the world where they lived . . . when rewriting is impossible, selection seems desirable.'

And he went on to say: 'In principle I think a *Collected Poems* should offer everything one has written. In practice I have excluded most of the last 14 pages of *A Time to Dance,* and all but two choruses of *Noah and the Waters.* Cuts might well have been made, too, in the first three books, particularly *The Magnetic Mountain.*'

I agree, and this is the justification of the procedure I have adopted.

It is time now to take a closer look at Day Lewis's achievement as a whole. And since it seemed to me sensible to arrange the poems chronologically, so as to bring out the marked manner in which (unlike some of his contemporaries) he developed poetically as well as stylistically, let us begin at the beginning. As I have said, he started writing poetry very young, and two small volumes of verse — *Beechen Vigil* and *Country Comets* — had been accepted before he left Oxford. They were apprentice work, but I have chosen three poems from them to illustrate the unusually assured command of tone and technique which they evinced.

Day Lewis then went on to write the three verse sequences — *Transitional Poem* (1929), *From Feathers to Iron* (1931) and *The Magnetic Mountain* (1933) — on which his reputation as a representative poet of the 'thirties was largely based. Looking back on them now, after more than forty years, I am struck anew by the freshness of their approach both to personal and to contemporary problems, the vigour of their language, and their rhythmical variety. In them were deployed for the first time the succinctness of:

> Somewhere beyond the railheads
> Of reason, south or north,
> Lies a magnetic mountain
> Riveting sky to earth.
>
> No line is laid so far.
> Ties rusting in a stack
> And sleepers — dead men's bones —
> Mark a defeated track.

and the parallel adroitness of:

> But Two there are, shadow us everywhere
> And will not let us be till we are dead,
> Hardening the bones, keeping the spirit spare,
> Original in water, earth and air,
> Our bitter cordial, our daily bread.

But they were still inescapably works of promise rather than achievement, works in which the poet's intellectual aplomb and technical virtuosity were to some extent developed at the expense of emotional intensity.

With *A Time to Dance* and *Noah and the Waters* Day Lewis moved away from writing poetry out of his personal relationships: his first marriage and its aftermath (though these remained seminal experiences which subsequently inspired some of his most deeply felt and moving poems), and wrote a more 'public' kind of poetry in which he sought to give expression to the aspirations of the young left-wing writers and thinkers with whom he had so much sympathy. It was not an easy thing to do, and neither book added much to the reputation he had already achieved; but *A Time to Dance* did contain two or three poems — 'The Conflict', 'Losers' and 'In Me Two Worlds' — that poignantly convey the plight of the underdog in a stratified society, and reflect not only Day Lewis's growing concern for humanity, but also, more important for his poetry, his increasing sense of the tug and tension between the past he had inherited and the future he so passionately hoped to see come about.

It was in *Overtures to Death* and *Word Over All* that Day Lewis first attempted to give concrete expression to the deeper, more pessimistic feelings underlying his political philosophy. The threat of another war was already on the horizon when he asked:

> Whether to die,
> Or live beneath fear's eye —
> Heavily hangs the sentence of this sky.

and looked back nostalgically to the time when:

> We who in younger days,
> Hoping too much, tried on
> The habit of perfection,
> Have learnt how it betrays.

And though the major poem from which *Overtures to Death* takes its title has certain longueurs (which is why I have omitted two of its seven sections) it is nevertheless a remarkably sustained performance, varying in tone from the pithiness of:

> You were the one our parents
> Could not forget or forgive —
> A remittance man, a very very
> Distant relative.

to the more sombre utterance of:

> Now we at last have crossed the line
> Where earth's exuberant fields begin,
> That green illusion in the sky
> Born of our desert years can die.

This is perhaps the right point at which to talk about the poets who influenced Day Lewis. They were many, and not all of them beneficial. Hardy, of course, is the first who comes to mind; but nobody reading the poems Day Lewis wrote during and immediately after his years at Oxford could fail to notice the pervading influence of W. H. Auden at that time:

> Green fields were my slippers,
> Sky was my hat,
> But curiosity
> Killed the cat.
> For this did I burst
> My daisy band —
> To be clapped in irons
> By a strange hand?

There is no mistaking the provenance of that, and indeed Day Lewis himself has told us that 'Wystan roused to its utmost my emulative faculty.'* Oddly enough, though, his influence was not wholly a bad one. Strictly contemporaneous influences, as opposed to more remote ones, often are not. And I am inclined to believe that some at least of Day Lewis's Audenesque poems of this period are at least as good as, if not rather better than, their stylistic originals. At all events, within two or three years Day Lewis had got the smartness that rubbed off on him from Auden out of his system and was writing a different kind of poetry:

> Mother earth, understand me. You send up
> So many leaves to meet the light,
> So many flights of birds,
> That keep you all their days in shade and song;
> And the blown leaf is part of you again
> And the frozen blackbird falls into your breast.

Some of it was narrative verse, of which he wrote a great deal. And though none of this, except possibly certain sections of *An Italian Visit,* can in my view be counted among his best work, it is never feeble, almost always technically accomplished, and sometimes brilliant — as in the splendidly evocative description of the moment of take-off which opens the section called 'Flight to Italy'.

Another poet, whose influence though less emphatic was unquestionably baneful, is Gerard Manley Hopkins. In the 'thirties, of course, it was virtually impossible *not* to be influenced by him, at least to some extent. Hopkins was very much 'in the air' and indeed part of the contemporary literary scene. But his manner is so idiosyncratic, and his complex rhythms so intrinsically part of it, that he was a very bad model. Day Lewis made several attempts to assimilate him but never succeeded, and lines like:

> Is it your hope, hope's hearth, heart's home, here at the
> lane's end?

*The Buried Day, Chatto & Windus, London, 1960; p. 178.

or:

> Praise wild, tame, common rare — chrysanthemums

betray their origin unequivocally. No less unequivocally than:

> From husk of words unspoken
> I'll winnow a ripe seed:
> From woods where love was shy to trespass
> I'll learn the airs I need.

which clearly owes something to A.E. Housman. Nevertheless his Songs in frank imitation of Jane Elliot's 'Lament for Flodden' or Marlow's 'The Passionate Shepherd', and the pastiche send-ups of contemporary poets in Part Five of *An Italian Visit,* have an admirable edge and point.

Much more potent and productive was the influence of two poets with whom Day Lewis had much in common, both as a man and as a maker of verse: Hardy and Edward Thomas. The reason is plain. Although Day Lewis was obliged to spend the greater part of his adult life in towns, he remained a countryman at heart. The look of the landscape, the changing movement of clouds, the rotation of crops and the comings and goings of bird, beast and flower were a perennial source of joy and inspiration to him. They informed a large part of his poetry, and it was only natural that in writing about them he should echo some of the distinctive tone, the unstressed almost colloquial rhythm, that characterize Edward Thomas's poems, which he knew intimately and rightly admired. The result was nearly always successful, as in 'Seen From the Train' or 'The Gate'.

With Hardy it was different. Here it was less a question of a common interest than of a common mode of feeling. Day Lewis was steeped in Hardy from an early age, spent the formative years of his life in Dorset, and never lost his love for that beguiling countryside. But affinity of feeling is different from an affinity of subject-matter, and though Hardy is behind much of the very best that Day Lewis wrote, particularly in the elegiac vein of 'Cornet Solo', he was sometimes too positively present, as in 'The House-Warming'.

In the early 1960s Day Lewis turned his attention to the dramatic monologue, a verse form to which he was no doubt attracted through his interest in Browning. In *The Gate* he published two such pieces: 'The Disabused' and 'Not Proven'. The former is an imagined self-inquisition by a man who, forty years earlier when scarcely more than a schoolboy, had through the paralysis of fear let his elder brother drown. It is very well done from a psychological point of view, but poetically it seems to me a little forced, a shade melodramatic; and definitely inferior to 'Not Proven', which I have therefore preferred. The latter is a remarkable tour-de-force on the subject of Madeleine Smith, the Scotswoman tried for muder in 1857 who lived on to be 92, and anybody who was lucky enough to hear Dame Peggy Ashcroft reading — or it might be more accurate to say impersonating — the part of Madeleine will know the poem's immense dramatic potential.

Day Lewis was an active translator of both Latin and French poetry, and I have therefore thought it right to include some examples of his work in this field. The major part of it comprised renderings of Virgil, whose *Georgics* (1940), *Aeneid* (1952) and *Eclogues* (1963) he translated *in toto*. The Foreword to his version of the *Aeneid* makes it plain that he was well aware of the difficulties confronting him when he accepted the BBC's commission to undertake the work. He spelt out there the crucial problem, which was not how to put into English what Virgil said, but how he said it; and the related problem of finding both a contemporary equivalent of Virgil's language — the richness and complexity of its texture — and a metre that would allow a faithful line-for-line translation without involving either omissions or padding. He reckoned that he had found it in a line with 6 stresses, which would accommodate anything from 12 to 17 syllables, and he proceeded to use this in all three Virgil books. Of their faithfulness to the originals I am not qualified to speak, but I am very willing to accept the verdict of the many distinguished classical scholars who praised their accuracy. In the *Aeneid*, especially, I think the result is decidedly impressive, not only for the vitality and appropriateness of its language, but for its sustained narrative pace. This is not something easy to achieve in an epic of roughly 10,000 lines. I am less happy about the 6-stress metre, which (as Day Lewis himself admitted) could not encompass 'the melodic variety and the complexity of rhythm' which Virgil achieved within the Latin hexameter. That is certainly true, as a comparison of any well-known line with its English counterpart will show. The sense of:

Tendebantque manūs, ripae ulterioris amore

is aptly rendered by:

Their hands stretched out in longing for the shore
beyond the river

but not the rhythmical sublimity of Virgil's line. That is perhaps an acceptable price to pay for translations that are linguistically accurate, faithful to their originals in spirit, mood, and above all tone, and yet unmistakably contemporary. It was only in seeking rather too zealously to prevent his radio listeners' attention from flagging by 'introducing here and there a sharp bold colloquialism' that Day Lewis occasionally lapsed into anachronistic comicalities.

Of his translations from the French, his rendering of Valéry's *Le Cimetière marin* seems to me outstanding, and I have included it entire. To translate such a complex, symbolical and highly imaginative poem into another language is an almost impossible task: to produce a version that is a poem in its own right is surely a triumph.

In 1968 Day Lewis succeeded John Masefield as Poet Laureate. It was an appointment which did him honour, but was of no service to his poetry. Being a conscientious man he conceived it his duty to try to fulfil the obligations of the office — obligations which few of his predecessors (with the possible exception of Dryden) had discharged with any credit, and which some of them resolutely declined to attempt. It might have been better if Day Lewis had followed the latters' example, for writing *vers d'occasion* was not his forte. Poems written to celebrate the Queen's return from an overseas tour, or the investiture of the young Prince of Wales, were banal when they were not embarrassingly ingenuous. However, since this book attempts to reflect every aspect of Day Lewis's work I have included in the final section three or four examples of these 'official' poems which seem to me as accomplished as such things ever can be. And here I must confess to having printed only the first two verses of 'Battle of Britain', a poem written for the première of the film of that name, because they strike me as so much more succinct and compelling than the remaining verses. I hope I may be forgiven for this editorial latitude.

I have said nothing so far about the quality which I imagine readers would regard as the most noteworthy in Day Lewis: his passionate interest in form. He was a very widely read man, not only in French and English literature but also in the classics, which he studied at Sherborne, where he was a scholar, and later at Oxford, where as an Exhibitioner at Wadham he came under the influence of Maurice Bowra. In these diverse literatures he discovered the multiplicity of forms in which poetry can be written, and was captivated by them. As Roy Fuller has truly said: 'He was always trying out stanza forms, rhymes and half-rhymes, the alternation of long and short lines.' In the process he developed a technique of great virtuosity, which sometimes led him astray but more often enabled him to say rather complicated things with admirable precision, and to convey moods and feelings of much subtlety with an enviable discrimination. A poet of the heart rather than the head, his feelings were never far below the surface, not at all because they were shallow in themselves but because his emotional antennae responded quickly to any stimulus. The poems which resulted were sometimes insufficiently digested, and occasionally altogether too 'personal' in a limiting sense. As he himself said: 'However intimate the experience out of which we write, in the act of making a poem from it, that experience must be distanced.' Here his technical assurance came to his aid, for it imposed on poems otherwise at risk a formal elegance which in itself was a distancing factor. Two of his most moving personal poems, 'Getting Warm — Getting Cold' and 'Walking Away', exemplify the point. Both of them are about incidents in the childhood of his daughter and eldest son, and both tremble on the brink of, and yet miraculously escape, the pitfall I have described.

Elsewhere, and I am thinking particularly of some of his lyric and elegiac poems, no such reservations are necessary. Take, for example, the short lyric called 'This Loafer' from *The Room*:

> In a sun-crazed orchard
> Busy with blossomings
> This loafer, unaware of
> What toil or weather brings,
> Lumpish sleeps — a chrysalis
> Waiting, no doubt, for wings.
>
> And when he does get active,
> It's not for business — no
> Bee-lines to thyme or heather,
> No earnest to-and-fro
> Of thrushes: pure caprice tells him
> Where and how to go.
>
> All he can ever do,
> Is to be entrancing,
> So that a child may think,
> Upon a chalk-blue chancing,
> 'Today was special. I met
> A piece of the sky dancing.'

And in the same form, though in a very different vein, he could also write, in 'Elegy for a Woman Unknown', these intensely compelling lines:

> At her charmed height of summer —
> Prospects, children rosy,
> In the heart's changeful music
> Discords near resolved —
> Her own flesh turned upon her:
> The gross feeder slowly
> Settled to consume her.

In them, one can surely say, art and artifice, thought and feeling, have come together in a creative fusion.

Day Lewis wrote a number of poems of this calibre, as I hope this book will show. They may not be all that numerous, but how many poets have produced more than a handful of enduring poems? Tennyson, with whom Day Lewis had much in common, is remembered for not very many poems, scattered through the works of a lifetime. But which of us would be without 'Ulysses', 'Tithonus', or the great passages from 'In Memoriam'? So with Day Lewis. His most memorable poems are embedded in a large body of work, which ranges from pure lyrics like 'Statuette: Late Minoan' or 'Love was once light as air', through deft exercises like 'Apollonian Figure' and 'Final Instructions', to much more ambitious poems, some of which are at least comparable with his best. In addition to those I have already cited or quoted from, 'The Christmas Tree', 'On Not Saying Everything', 'At Old Head, Co. Mayo' and the superlative 'Pegasus' spring to mind. In any case I cherish a firm conviction that Thomas Hardy, close to whose grave in Stinsford churchyard Day Lewis lies buried, will not have been backward in welcoming him to the Elysian fields.

I.M.P.

Early Poems
From Beechen Vigil (1925)
and Country Comets (1928)

Words

Were I this forest pool
And you the birch tree bending over,
Your thoughts in shaken leaves could drop
Upon my heart. And we would never
So fret our happiness taming
Rebellious words that sulk, run crazy
And gibber like caged monkeys,
Mocking their tamers.

Between Hush and Hush

Dear, do not think that I
Will praise your beauty the less,
Believing death for ever
Snows up its fair impress.

Nor slight my love because
It claims no magic re-birth,
But deems all kissing over
When lips are laid to earth.

I'll praise your beauty as
A dewdrop fast on its prime —
A still perfection lasting
But for one blink of time.

So short its hour, your love
To mine should bravelier rush,
Bird-note to bird-note thrusting
Out between hush and hush.

The Perverse

Love being denied, he turned in his despair
And couched with the Absolute a summer through;
He got small joy of the skimpy bedfellow —
Formulas gave no body to lay bare.

His pretty came among the primroses
With open breast for him. No more denied
Seemed no more ideal. He was unsatisfied
Till he strained her flesh to thin philosophies.

Love being remote, dreams at the midnight gave
A chill enchanted image of her flesh;
Such phantoms but inflamed his waking wish
For the quick beauty no dream-chisels grave.

Now she was won. But our Pygmalion —
If so he could have graven like a kiss
On Time's blank shoulder that hour of loveliness
— He would have changed her body into stone.

From Transitional Poem (1929)

To Rex Warner

Transitional Poem

Part One

Ira brevis, longa est pietas, recidiva voluptas;
Et cum posse perit, mens tamen una manet.

MAXIMIAN

1

Now I have come to reason
And cast my schoolboy clout,
Disorder I see is without,
And the mind must sweat a poison
Keener than Thessaly's brew;
A pus that, discharged not thence,
Gangrenes the vital sense
And makes disorder true.
It is certain we shall attain
No life till we stamp on all
Life the tetragonal
Pure symmetry of brain.

I felt, in my scorning
Of common poet's talk,
As arrogant as the hawk
When he mounts above the morning.
'Behold man's droll appearance,
Faith wriggling upon his hooks,
Chin-deep in Eternal Flux
Angling for reassurance!'
I care not if he retorts —
'Of all that labour and wive
And worship, who would give
A fiddlestick for these thoughts
That sluggishly yaw and bend,

Fat strings of barges drawn
By a tug they have never seen
And never will comprehend?'

I sit in a wood and stare
Up at untroubled branches
Locked together and staunch as
Though girders of the air:
And think, the first wind rising
Will crack that intricate crown
And let the daylight down.
But there is naught surprising
Can explode the single mind: —
Let figs from thistles fall
Or stars from their pedestal,
This architecture will stand.

2

Come, soul, let us not fight
Like cynical Chinee
Beneath umbrella, nor wish to trade
Upon neutrality.
For the mind must cope with
All elements or none —
Bask in dust along with weevils,
Or criticize the sun.

Look, where cloud squadrons are
Stampeded by the wind,
A boy's kite sits as calm as Minos
If the string be sound:
But if there are no hands
To keep the cable tense
And no eyes to mark a flaw in it,
What use the difference
Between a gust that twitters

Along the wainscot at dawn
And a burly wind playing the zany
In fields of barleycorn?

The time has gone when we
Could sprawl at ease between
Light and darkness, and deduce
Omnipotence from our Mean.
For us the gregorian
Example of those eyes
That risked hell's blight and heaven's blinding
But dared not compromise.

3

That afternoon we lay on Lillington Common
The land wallowed around us in the sunlight;
But finding all things my strenuous sense included
Ciphers new-copied by the indefinite sunlight,
I fell once more under the shadow of my Sphinx.
The aimlessness of buttercup and beetle
So pestered me, I would have cried surrender
To the fossil certitudes of Tom, Dick, and Harry,
Had I known how or believed that such a surrender
Could fashion aught but a dead Sphinx from the live Sphinx.
Later we lit a fire, and the hedge of darkness —
Garnished with not a nightingale nor a glow-worm —
Sprang up like the beanstalk by which our Jack aspired once.
Then, though each star seemed little as a glow-worm
Perched on Leviathan's flank, and equally terrible
My tenure of this plateau that sloped on all sides
Into annihilation — yet was I lord of
Something: for, seeing the fall of a burnt-out faggot
Make all the night sag down, I became lord of
Light's interplay — stoker of an old parable.

4

Come up, Methuselah,
You doddering superman!
Give me an instant realized
And I'll outdo your span.

In that one moment of evening
When roses are most red
I can fold back the firmament,
I can put time to bed.

Abraham, stint your tally
Of concubines and cattle!
Give place to me — capitalist
In more intrinsic metal.

I have a lover of flesh
And a lover that is a sprite:
Today I lie down with finite,
Tomorrow with infinite.

That one is a constant
And suffers no eclipse,
Though I feel sun and moon burning
Together on her lips.

This one is a constant,
But she's not kind at all;
She raddles her gown with my despairs
And paints her lip with gall.

My lover of flesh is wild,
And willing to kiss again;
She is the potency of earth
When woods exhale the rain.

My lover of air, like Artemis
Spectrally embraced,
Shuns the daylight that twists her smile
To mineral distaste.

Twin poles energic, they
Stand fast and generate
This spark that crackles in the void
As between fate and fate.

          *   *   *

7

Few things can more inflame
This far too combative heart
Than the intellectual Quixotes of the age
Prattling of abstract art.
No one would deny it —
But for a blind man's passion
Cassandra had been no more than a draggle-skirt,
Helen a ten-year fashion.
Yet had there not been one hostess
Ever whose arms waylaid
Like the tough bramble a princeling's journey, or
At the least no peasant maid
Redressing with rude heat
Nature's primeval wrong,
Epic had slumbered on beneath his blindness
And Helen lacked her song.

(So the antique balloon
Wobbles with no defence
Against the void but a grapnel that hops and ploughs
Through the landscape of sense.)

Phrase-making, dress-making —
Distinction's hard to find;

For thought must play the mannequin, strut in phrase,
Or gape with the ruck: and mind,
Like body, from covering gets
Most adequate display.
Yet time trundles this one to the rag-and-bone man,
While that other may
Reverberate all along
Man's craggy circumstance —
Naked enough to keep its dignity
Though it eye God askance.

Part Two

Do I contradict myself?
Very well then, I contradict myself;
I am large, I contain multitudes.

WALT WHITMAN

* * *

9

I thought to have had some fame
As the village idiot
Condemned at birth to sit
Oracle of blind alleys:
Shanghaied aboard the galleys
I got reprieve and shame.

Tugging at his oar
This idiot who, for lack
Of the striped Zodiac,
Swore that every planet
Was truck, soon found some merit
In his own abject star.

Then there came disgust
Of the former loon who could
Elbow a bridge and brood
From Chaos to last Trump
Over the imbecile pomp
Of waters dribbling past.

For what can water be
But so much less or more
Gravamen to the oar? —
(Reasons our reformed dunce)'
It is high time to renounce
This village idiocy.

10

How they would jeer at us —
Ulysses, Herodotus,
The hard-headed Phoenicians
Or, of later nations,
Columbus, the Pilgrim Fathers
And a thousand others
Who laboured only to find
Some pittance of new ground,
Merchandize or women.
Those rude and bourgeois seamen
Got glory thrown in
As it were with every ton
Of wave that swept their boat,
And would have preferred a coat
For keeping off the spray.

Since the heroes lie
Entombed with the recipe
Of epic in their heart,
And have buried — it seems — that art
Of minding one's own business
Magnanimously, for us

There's nothing but to recant
Ambition, and be content
Like the poor child at play
To find a holiday
In the sticks and mud
Of a familiar road.

11

If I bricked up ambition and gave no air
To the ancestral curse that gabbles there,
 I could leave wonder on the latch
 And with a whole heart watch
The calm declension of an English year.

I would be pedagogue — hear poplar, lime
And oak recite the seasons' paradigm.
 Each year a dynasty would fall
 Within my orchard wall —
I'd be their Tacitus, and they my time.

Among those pippin princes I could ease
A heart long sick for some Hesperides:
 Plainsong of thrushes in the soul
 Would drown that rigmarole
Of Eldorados, Auks, and Perilous Seas.

(The God they cannot see sages define
In a slow-motion. If I discipline
 My flux into a background still
 And sure as a waterfall
Will not a rainbow come of that routine?)

So circumscribe the vampire and he'll die soon —
Lunacy and anaemia take their own.
 Grounded in temperate soil I'll stay,
 An orchard god, and say
My glow-worms hold a candle to the moon.

Enough. There is no magic
Circle nor prophylactic
Sorcery of garlic
Will keep the vampire in.
See! — that authentic
Original of sin
Slides from his cabin
Up to my sober trees
And spits disease.
Thus infected, they
Start a sylvan rivalry,
Poplar and oak surpass
Their natural green, and race
Each other to the stars.

Since my material
Has chosen to rebel,
It were most politic —
Ere I also fall sick —
To escape this Eden.
Indeed there has been no peace
For any garden
Or for any trees
Since Priapus died,
And lust can no more ride
Over self-love and pride.

Leave Eden to the brutes:
For he who lets his sap
Run downward to the roots
Will wither at the top
And wear fool's-cap.
I am no English lawn
To build a smooth tradition
Out of Time's recession
And centuries of dew . . .

Adam must subdue
The indestructible serpent,
Outstaring it: content
If he can transplant
One slip from paradise
Into his own eyes.

* * *

14

In heaven, I suppose, lie down together
Agonized Pilate and the boa-constrictor
That swallows anything: but we must seize
One horn or the other of our antitheses.
When I consider each independent star
Wearing its world of darkness like a fur
And rubbing shoulders with infinity,
I am content experience should be
More discontinuous than the points pricked
Out by the mazy course of a derelict,
Iceberg, or Flying Dutchman, and the heart
Stationary and passive as a chart.
In such star-frenzy I could boast, betwixt
My yester and my morrow self are fixed
All the birds carolling and all the seas
Groaning from Greenwich to the Antipodes.

But an eccentric hour may come, when systems
Not stars divide the dark; and then life's pistons
Pounding into their secret cylinder
Begin to tickle the most anchorite ear
With hints of mechanisms that include
The man. And once that rhythm arrests the blood,
Who would be satisfied his mind is no
Continent but an archipelago?
They are preposterous paladins and prance
From myth to myth, who take an Agag stance

Upon the needle points of here and now,
Where only angels ought to tread. Allow
One jointure feasible to man, one state
Squared with another — then he can integrate
A million selves and where disorder ruled
Straddle a chaos and beget a world.

Peals of the New Year once for me came tumbling
Out of the narrow night like clusters of humming-
Birds loosed from a black bag, and rose again
Irresponsibly to silence: but now I strain
To follow them and see for miles around
Men square or shrug their shoulders at the sound.
Then I remember the pure and granite hills
Where first I caught an ideal tone that stills,
Like the beloved's breath asleep, all din
Of earth at traffic: silence's first-born,
Carrying over each sensual ravine
To inform the seer and uniform the seen.
So from this ark, this closet of the brain,
The dove emerges and flies back again
With a Messiah sprig of certitude —
Promise of ground below the sprawling flood.

15

Desire is a witch
And runs against the clock.
It can unstitch
The decent hem
Where space tacks on to time:
It can unlock
Pandora's privacies.

It puffs in these
Top-gallants of the mind,
And away I stand
On the elemental gale

Into an ocean
That the liar Lucian
Had never dared retail.

When my love leans with all
Her shining breast and shoulder,
I know she is older
Than Ararat the hill,
And yet more young
Than the first daffodil
That ever shews a spring.

When her eyes delay
On me, so deep are they
Tunnelled by love, although
You poured Atlantic
In this one and Pacific
In the other, I know
They would not overflow.

Desire clicks back
Like cuckoo into clock;
Leaves me to explain
Eyes that a tear will drown
And a body where youth
Nor age will long remain
To implicate the truth.

It seems that we must call
Anything truth whose well
Is deep enough;
For the essential
Philosopher-stone, desire,
Needs no other proof
Than its own fire.

      *   *   *

When nature plays hedge-schoolmaster,
Shakes out the gaudy map of summer
And shows me charabanc, rose, barley-ear
And every bright-winged hummer,

He only would require of me
To be the sponge of natural laws
And learn no more of that cosmography
Than passes through the pores.

Why must I then unleash my brain
To sweat after some revelation
Behind the rose, heedless if truth maintain
On the rose-bloom her station?

When bullying April bruised mine eyes
With sleet-bound appetites and crude
Experiments of green, I still was wise
And kissed the blossoming rod.

Now summer brings what April took,
Riding with fanfares from the south,
And I should be no Solomon to look
My Sheba in the mouth.

Charabancs shout along the lane
And summer gales bay in the wood
No less superbly because I can't explain
What I have understood.

Let logic analyse the hive,
Wisdom's content to have the honey:
So I'll go bite the crust of things and thrive
While hedgerows still are sunny.

Part Three

*But even so, amid the tornadoed Atlantic of
my being, do I myself still centrally disport
in mute calm.*
HERMAN MELVILLE

18

On my right are trees and a lank stream sliding
Impervious as Anaconda to the suns
Of autumn; and the boughs are vipers writhing
To slough the summer from their brittle bones.
Here is the Trojan meadow, here Scamander;
And I, the counterfeit Achilles, feel
A river-god surge up to tear me asunder,
A serpent melancholy bruise my heel.

On my left is the city famed for talk
And tolerance. Its old men run about
Chasing reality, chasing the Auk
With butterfly-nets. Its young men swell the rout
Gaping at Helen in the restaurant,
Mocking at Helen from monastic towers.
Boy Achilles, who has known Helen too long
To scold or worship, stands outside and glowers.

Between the stream and city a rubbish heap
Proclaims the pleasant norm with smouldering stenches.
See! the pathetic pyre where Trojans keep
Well out of sight the prey of time's revenges;
Old butterfly-nets, couches where lovers lay —
All furniture out of fashion. So the fire
Guts the proud champions of the real: so Troy
Cremates her dead selves and ascends to higher.

Grecians awake, salute the happy norm!
Now may Achilles find employment still;
And once again the blood-lust will grow warm,
Gloating on champions he could never kill.
And if Scamander rears up and pursues,
This ring of rubbish fire will baffle all
His rage. Hero, you're safe, in the purlieus
Of God's infernal acre king and thrall.

19

When April comes alive
Out of the small bird's throat,
Achilles in the sunshine
Kept on his overcoat.
Trojan and Greek at battle,
Helen wantoning —
None but heroic metal
Could ignore the spring.

When honeysuckle and summer
Suffocate the lane,
That sulky boil was broken
And I at last a man.
I'd have stripped off my skin to
The impacts of hate and love —
Rebel alone because I
Could not be slave enough.

Bodies now, not shadows,
Intercept the sun:
It takes no rod to tell me
That discipline's begun.
Seeking the fabled fusion
From love's last chemical,
I found the experiment
Makes monads of us all;

For love still keeps apart,
And all its vanities
But emphasize higher heaven,
As February trees
When rooks begin their noisy
Coronation of the wood
Are turreted with folly
Yet grow toward some good.

I thought, since love can harness
Pole with contrary pole,
It must be earthed in darkness
Deeper than mine or mole.
Now that I have loved
A while and not gone blind,
I think love's terminals
Are fixed in fire and wind.

20

How often, watching the windy boughs
Juggle with the moon, or leaning
My body against a wind
That sets all earth careening;
Or when I have seen flames browsing
On the prairie of night and tossing
Their muzzles up at Orion;
Or the sun's hot arsenal spent
On a cloud salient
Till the air explodes with light;
How often have I perceived a delight
Which parallels the racing mind,
But never rides it off the course.

Another fire, another wind
Now take the air, and I
Am matched with a stricter ecstasy.
For he whom love and fear enlist

To comb his universe
For what Protagoras missed,
Needs be reborn hermaphrodite
And put himself out to nurse
With a siren and a sibyl.
So the spider gradually,
Drawing fine systems from his belly,
Includes creation with a thread
And squats on the navel of his world.
Yet even that arch-fakir must feed
Austerity on warm blood.

The tracks of love and fear
Lead back till I disappear
Into that ample terminus
From which all trains draw out
Snorting towards an Ultima Thule.
Nothing is altered about
The place, except its gloom is newly
Lacquered by an unaccustomed eye,
Yet cannot blunt mine eyes now
To the clear finality
Of all beginnings.
         Outside
In the diamond air of day
The engines simmer with delay,
Desiring a steely discipline
No less, though now quite satisfied
They travel a loop-line.

21

My lover is so happy, you well might say
One of the Hellene summers had lost its way
And taken shelter underneath her breast.
None but its proper fear can now arrest
Our meteoric love: but still we grieve
That curves of mind and body should outlive

All expectation, and the heart become
A blunt habitual arc, a pendulum
Wagged by the ghost of its first impetus.
Love keeps the bogey slave to admonish us
Of vanity, yet through this fear we scrawl
Our sky with love's vain comets ere it fall.

And then, up on High Stoy standing alone,
We saw the excellence of the serious down
That shakes the seasons from its back, and bears
No obligation but to wind and stars.
What paroxysm of green can crack those huge
Ribs grown from Chaos, stamped by the Deluge?

Later, within the wood sweetly reclining
On bluebell and primrose, we loved; whose shining
Made a poor fiction of the royal skies,
But were to love alone repositories
Of what by-product wonder it could spare
From lips and eyes. Yet nothing had such power
As prattle of small flowers within the brake
To mount the panic heart and rein it back
From the world's edge. For they, whose virtue lies
In a brief act of beauty, summarize
Earth's annual passion and leave the naked earth
Still dearer by their death than by their birth.
So we, who are love's hemispheres hiding
Beneath the coloured ordeal of our spring,
Shall be disclosed, and I shall see your face
An autumn evening certain of its peace.

22

It is an easier thing
To give up great possessions
Than to forego one farthing
Of the rare unpossessed.

But I've been satellite
Long enough to this moon,
The pharisee of night
Shining by tradition.

There's no star in the sky
But gazing makes it double
And the infatuate eye
Can breed dilemmas on it.

Wiser it were to sheath
My burning heart in clay
Than by this double breath
To magnify the tomb.

I'd live like grass and trees,
Familiar of the earth,
Proving its basalt peace
Till I was unperturbed

By synod of the suns
Or a moon's insolence
As the ant when he runs
Beneath sky-scraping grass.

23

You've trafficked with no beast but unicorn
Who dare hold me in scorn
For my dilemmas. Nor have you perceived
The compass-point suggest
An east by pointing to the west,
Or you'd not call me thus deceived
For fixing my desire
On this magnetic north to gyre
Under the sheer authority of ice.

24

I have seen what impertinence
Stokes up the dingy rhetoric of sense:
I've seen your subaltern ambitions rise
Yellow and parallel
As smoke from garden cities that soon fades
In air it cannot even defile. Poor shades,
Not black enough for hell,
Learn of this poplar which beyond its height
Aspires not, and will bend beneath the thumb
Of every wind; yet when the stars come
It is an omen darker than the night.

The rest may go. No satisfaction lies
In such. And you alone shall hear
My pride, whose love's the accurate frontier
Of all my enterprise.
While your beauties' succession
Holds my adventure in a flowery chain
As the spring hedgerows hold the lane,
How can I care whether it ends upon
Marsh or metropolis?

But look within my heart, see there
The tough stoic ghost of a pride was too severe
To risk an armistice
With lesser powers than death; but rather died
Welcoming that iron in the soul
Which keeps the spirit whole,
Since none but ghosts are satisfied
To see a glory passing and let it pass.
For I had been a modern moth and hurled
Myself on many a flaming world,
To find its globe was glass.
In you alone
I met the naked light, by you became
Veteran of a flame
That burns away all but the warrior bone.
And I shall know, if time should falsify

This star the company of my night,
Mine is the heron's flight
Which makes a solitude of any sky.

24

Farewell again to this adolescent moon;
        I say it is a bottle
For papless poets to feed their fancy on.
        Once mine sucked there, and I dreamed
The heart a record for the gramophone —
        One scratch upon the surface,
And the best music of that sphere is gone.
        So I put passion away
In a cold storage and took its tune on trust,
        While proper men with church-bells
Signal a practised or a dreamt-of lust . . .
        No fear could sublimate
The ennui of a tomb where music slept
        In artificial frost,
Nor could it long persuade me to accept
        Rigidity for peace.
Moon-stricken I worked out a solitude
        Of sand and sun, believing
No other soil could bear the genuine rood.
        But nothing grew except
The shadow at my heels. Now I confess
        There's no virtue in sand:
It is the rose that makes the wilderness.

        I thought integrity
Needed a desert air; I saw it plain,
        A chimney of stone at evening,
A monolith on the skyline after rain.
        Instead, the witless sun
Fertilized that old succubus and bred
        A skeleton in a shadow.

Let cactus spring where hermits go to bed
     With those they come to kill.
Three-legged I ran with that importunate curse,
     Till I guessed (in the sexual trance
Or playing darts with drunken schoolmasters)
     The integrity that's laid bare
Upon the edge of common furniture.
     Now to the town returning
I accept the blind collisions that ensure
     Soul's ektogenesis.

25

Where is the true, the central stone
That clay and vapour zone,
That earthquakes budge nor vinegar bites away,
That rivets man against Doomsday?

You will not find it there, although
You sink a shaft below
Despair and see the roots of death close-curled
About the kernel of your world.

Where is the invaluable star
Whose beams enlacèd are
The scaffolding of truth, whose stages drawn
Aside unshutter an ideal dawn?

It is well hid. You would not find
It there, though far you mined
Up through the golden seams that cram the night
And walked those galleries of light.

Above, below, the Flux tight-packed
Stages its sexual act —
An ignominious scuffling in the dark
Where brute encounters brute baresark.

Keep to the pithead, then, nor pry
Beyond what meets the eye,
Since household stuff, stone walls, mountains and trees
Placard the day with certainties.

For individual truth must lie
Within diversity;
Under the skin all creatures are one race,
Proved integers but by their face.

So he, who learns to comprehend
The form of things, will find
They in his eye that purest star have sown
And changed his mind to singular stone.

26

Chiefly to mind appears
That hour on Silverhowe
When evening's lid hung low
And the sky was about our ears.
Buoyed between fear and love
We watched in eastward form
The armadas of the storm
And sail superbly above;
So near, they'd split and founder
On the least jag of sense,
One false spark fire the immense
Broadside the confounding thunder.
They pass, give not a salvo,
And in their rainy wash
We hear the horizons crash
With monitors of woe.

Only at highest power
Can love and fear become
Their equilibrium,
And in that eminent hour

A virtue is made plain
Of passionate cleavage
Like the hills' cutting edge
When the sun sets to rain.
This is the single mind,
This the star-solved equation
Of life with life's negation.
A deathless cell designed
To demonstrate death's act,
Which, the more surely it moves
To earth's influence, but proves
Itself the more intact.

27

With me, my lover makes
    The clock assert its chime:
But when she goes, she takes
    The mainspring out of time.

Yet this time-wrecking charm
    Were better than love dead
And its hollow alarum
    Hammered out on lead.

Why should I fear that Time
    Will superannuate
These workmen of my rhyme —
    Love, despair and hate?

Fleeing the herd, I came
    To a graveyard on a hill,
And felt its mould proclaim
    The bone gregarious still.

Boredoms and agonies
    Work out the rhythm of bone: —
No peace till creature his
    Creator has outgrown.

Passion dies from the heart
    But to infect the marrow;
Holds dream and act apart
    Till the man discard his narrow

Sapience and folly
    Here, where the graves slumber
In a green melancholy
    Of overblown summer.

Part Four

The hatches are let down
And the night meets the day
The spirit comes to its own
The beast to its play.

W. H. AUDEN

28

In the beginning was the Word.
    Under different skies now, I recall
    The childhood of the Word.
                          Before the Fall,
    Was dancing on the green with sun and moon:
And the Word was with God.
    Years pass, relaxed in a faun's afternoon.
And the Word was God.
    For him rise up the litanies of leaves

From the tormented wood, and semi-breves
Of birds accompany the simple dawn.
Obsequious to his mood the valleys yawn,
Nymphs scamper or succumb, waterfalls part
The hill-face with vivacious smiles. The heart,
Propped up against its paradise, records
Each wave of godhead in a sea of words.
He grows a wall of sunflower and moonflower blent
To protest his solitude and to prevent
Wolf or worm from trespassing on his rule.
Observe how paradise can make a fool:
They can't get in; but he — for a god no doubt
Is bound by his own laws — cannot get out.
And the Word was made flesh,
    Under different skies now,
    Wrenching a stony song from a scant acre,
    The Word still justifies its Maker.
        Green fields were my slippers,
           Sky was my hat,
        But curiosity
           Killed the cat.
        For this did I burst
           My daisy band —
        To be clapped in irons
           By a strange hand?
Nevertheless, you are well out of Eden:
For there's no wonder where all things are new;
No dream where all is sleep; no vision where
Seer and seen are one; nor prophecy
Where only echo waits upon the tongue.
    Now he has come to a country of stone walls,
Breathes a precarious air.
Frontiers of adamant declare
A cold autonomy. There echo starves;
And the mountain ash bleeds stoically there
Above the muscular stream.
What cairn will show the way he went?
A harrow rusting on defeated bones?

Or will he leave a luckier testament —
Rock deeply rent,
Fountains of spring playing upon the air?

* * *

30

In the chaotic age
   This was enough for me —
Her beauty walked the page
   And it was poetry.

Now that the crust has cooled,
   The floods are kept in pen,
Mountains have got their mould
   And air its regimen.

Nothing of heat remains
   But where the sacred hill
Conserves within her veins
   The fiery principle.

Fire can no longer shake
   Stars from their sockets down;
It burns now but to make
   Vain motions above the town.

This glum canal, has lain
   Opaque night after night,
One hour will entertain
   A jubilee of light,

And show that beauty is
   A motion of the mind
By its own dark caprice
   Directed or confined.

Where is the fool would want those days again
    Whose light was globed in pain
   And danced upon a point of wire?
   When the charged batteries of desire
    Had licence but to pass
Into a narrow room of frosted glass?

The globe was broken and the light made free
    Of a king's territory.
   Artemis then, that huntress pale,
   Flung her black dogs upon the trail:
    So with one glance around
The hunted lightning ran and went to ground.

Safer perhaps within that cell to stay
    Which qualified its ray
   And gave it place and period,
   Than be at liberty where God
    Has put no firmament
Of glass to prove dark and light different.

But Artemis leaps down. At her thin back
    Wheel the shades in a pack.
   At once that old habit of fire
   Jumps out, not stopping to inquire
    Whether it follows or flies,
Content to use the night for exercise.

And I, when at the sporting queen's halloo
    The light obedient flew
   Blazing its trail across the wild —
   Resigned now but not reconciled,
    That ancient Sphinx I saw
Put moon and shades like mice beneath its paw.

*   *   *

The hawk comes down from the air.
Sharpening his eye upon
A wheeling horizon
Turned scrutiny to prayer.

He guessed the prey that cowers
Below, and learnt to keep
The distance which can strip
Earth to its blank contours.

Then trod the air, content
With contemplation till
The truth of valley and hill
Should be self-evident.

Or as the little lark
Who veins the sky with song,
Asking from dawn to dark
No revenues of spring:

But with the night descends
Into his chosen tree,
And the famed singer ends
In anonymity.

So from a summer's height
I come into my peace;
The wings have earned their night,
And the song may cease.

From From Feathers to Iron (1931)

To The Mother

From Feathers to Iron

*Do thoughts grow like feathers, the dead end of
life?*
W. H. AUDEN

We take but three steps from feathers to iron.
JOHN KEATS

1

Suppose that we, tomorrow or the next day,
Came to an end — in storm the shafting broken,
Or a mistaken signal, the flange lifting —
Would that be premature, a text for sorrow?

Say what endurance gives or death denies us.
Love's proved in its creation, not eternity:
Like leaf or linnet the true heart's affection
Is born, dies later, asks no reassurance.

Over dark wood rises one dawn felicitous,
Bright through awakened shadows fall her crystal
Cadenzas, and once for all the wood is quickened.
So our joys visit us, and it suffices.

Nor fear we now to live who in the valley
Of the shadow of life have found a causeway;
For love restores the nerve and love is under
Our feet resilient. Shall we be weary?

Some say we walk out of Time altogether
This way into a region where the primrose
Shows an immortal dew, sun at meridian
Stands up for ever and in scent the lime tree.

This is a land which later we may tell of.
Here-now we know, what death cannot diminish
Needs no replenishing; yet certain are, though
Dying were well enough, to live is better.

Passion has grown full man by his first birthday.
Running across the bean-fields in a south wind,
Fording the river mouth to feel the tide-race —
Child's play that was, though proof of our possessions.

Now our research is done, measured the shadow,
The plains mapped out, the hills a natural boundary.
Such and such is our country. There remains to
Plough up the meadowland, reclaim the marshes.

                    *   *   *

3

            Back to the countryside
            That will not lose its pride
When the green flags of summer all are taken,
            Having no mind to force
            The seasons from their course
And no remorse for a front line forsaken.

            Look how the athletic field
            His flowery vest has peeled
To wrestle another fall with rain and sleet.
            The rock will not relent
            Nor desperate earth consent
Till the spent winter blows his long retreat.

            Come, autumn, use the spur!
            Let us not still defer
To drive slow furrows in the impatient soil:
            Persuade us now these last
            Silk summer shreds to cast
And fasten on the harsh habit of toil.

The swallows are all gone
Into the rising sun.
You leave tonight for the Americas.
Under the dropping days
Alone the labourer stays
And says that winter will be slow to pass.

* * *

5

Beauty's end is in sight,
Terminus where all feather joys alight.
Wings that flew lightly
Fold and are iron. We see
The thin end of mortality.

We must a little part,
And sprouting seed crack our cemented heart.
Who would get an heir
Initial loss must bear:
A part of each will be elsewhere.

What life may now decide
Is past the clutch of caution, the range of pride.
Speaking from the snow
The crocus lets me know
That there is life to come, and go.

6

Now she is like the white tree-rose
That takes a blessing from the sun:
Summer has filled her veins with light,
And her warm heart is washed with noon.

Or as a poplar, ceaselessly
Gives a soft answer to the wind:
Cool on the light her leaves lie sleeping,
Folding a column of sweet sound.

Powder the stars. Forbid the night
To wear those brilliants for a brooch
So soon, dark death, you may close down
The mines that made this beauty rich.

Her thoughts are pleiads, stooping low
O'er glades where nightingale has flown:
And like the luminous night around her
She has at heart a certain dawn.

*   *   *

8

He   We whom a full tornado cast up high,
        Two years marooned on self-sufficiency,
        Kissing on an island out of the trade-routes
        Nor glancing at horizon, — we'll not dare
        Outstay the welcome of our tropic sun.

She   Here is the dark Interior, noon yet high,
        Light to work by and a sufficiency
        Of timber. Build then. We may reach the trade-routes.
        We'll take the winds at their word; yes, will dare
        Wave's curling lip, the hot looks of the sun.

He   Hull is finished. Now must the foraging eye
        Take in provisions for a long journey:
        Put by our summertime, the fruits, the sweet roots,
        The virgin spring moss-shadowed near the shore,
        And over idle sands the halcyon.

She   No mark out there, no mainland meets the eye.
Horizon gapes; and yet must we journey
Beyond the bays of peace, pull up our sweet roots,
Cut the last cord links us to native shore,
Toil on waters too troubled for the halcyon.

Both   Though we strike a new continent, it shall be
Our islet; a new world, our colony.
If we miss land, no matter. We've a stout boat
Provisioned for some years: we need endure
No further ill than to be still alone.

*   *   *

10

Twenty weeks near past
Since the seed took to earth.
Winter has done his worst.
Let upland snow ignore;
Earth wears a smile betrays
What summer she has in store.
She feels insurgent forces
Gathering at the core,
And a spring rumour courses
Through her, till the cold extreme
Sleep of grove and grass is
Stirred, begins to dream.
So, when the violins gather
And soar to a final theme,
Broadcast on winds of ether
That golden seed extends
Beneath the sun-eye, the father,
To ear at the earth's ends.

11

There is a dark room,
The locked and shuttered womb,
Where negative's made positive.
Another dark room,
The blind, the bolted tomb,
Where positives change to negative.

We may not undo
That or escape this, who
Have birth and death coiled in our bones.
Nothing we can do
Will sweeten the real rue,
That we begin, and end, with groans.

* * *

13

But think of passion and pain.
Those absolute dictators will enchain
The low, exile the princely parts:
They close a door between the closest hearts:
Their verdict stands in steel,
From whose blank rigour kings may not appeal.

When in love's airs we'd lie,
Like elms we leaned together with a sigh
And sighing severed, and no rest
Had till that wind was past:
Then drooped in a green sickness over the plain
Wanting our wind again.

Now pain will come for you,
Take you into a desert without dew,
Labouring through the unshadowed day
To blast the sharp scarps, open up a way
There for the future line.
But I shall wait afar off and alone.

Small comfort may be found,
Though our embraced roots grope in the same ground;
Though on one permanent way we run,
Yes, under the same sun.
Contact the means, but travellers report
The ends are poles apart.

14

Now the full-throated daffodils,
Our trumpeters in gold,
Call resurrection from the ground
And bid the year be bold.

Today the almond tree turns pink,
The first flush of the spring;
Winds loll and gossip through the town
Her secret whispering.

Now too the bird must try his voice
Upon the morning air;
Down drowsy avenues he cries
A novel great affair.

He tells of royalty to be;
How with her train of rose
Summer to coronation comes
Through waving wild hedgerows.

Today crowds quicken in a street,
The fish leaps in the flood:
Look there, gasometer rises,
And here bough swells to bud.

For our love's luck, our stowaway,
Stretches in his cabin;
Our youngster joy barely conceived
Shows up beneath the skin.

Our joy was but a gusty thing
Without sinew or wit,
An infant flyaway; but now
We make a man of it.

15

I have come so far upon my journey.
This is the frontier, this is where I change,
And wait between two worlds to take refreshment.
    I see the mating plover at play
Blowing themselves about over the green wheat,
And in a bank I catch
The shy scent of the primrose that prevails
Strangely upon the heart. Here is
The last flutter of the wind-errant soul,
Earth's first faint tug at the earthbound soul.
    So, waiting here between winter and summer,
Conception and fruition, I
Take what refreshment may be had from skies
Uncertain as the wind, prepare
For a new route, a change of constitution.

Some change of constitution, where
Has been for years an indeterminate quarrel
Between a fevered head and a cold heart;

Rulers who cannot rule, rebels who will not
Rebel; an age divided
Between tomorrow's wink, yesterday's warning.
    And yet this self, contains
Tides continents and stars — a myriad selves,
Is small and solitary as one grass-blade
Passed over by the wind
Amongst a myriad grasses on the prairie.
    You in there, my son, my daughter,
Will you become dictator, resolve the factions?
Will you be my ambassador
And make my peace with the adjacent empires?

16

More than all else might you,
My son, my daughter,
Be metal to bore through
The impermeable clay
And rock that overlay
The living water.

Through that artesian well
Myself may out,
Finding its own level.
This way the waste land turns
To arable, and towns
Are rid of drought.

17

Down hidden causeways of the universe
Through space-time's cold
Indifferent airs I strolled,
A pointless star: till in my course
I happened on the sun
And in a spurt of fire to her did run.

That heavenly body as I neared began
To make response,
And heaved with fire at once.
One wave of gathered heat o'er-ran
Her all and came to a head,
A mountain based upon an ardent bed.

    (Faith may move mountains; but love's twice as strong,
For love can raise
A mountain where none was:
Also can prove astronomers wrong
Who deem the stars too hot
For life: — here is a star that has begot.)

Soon from the mother body torn and whirled
By tidal pull
And left in space to cool
That mountain top will be a world
Treading its own orbit,
And look to her for warmth, to me for wit.

18

It is time to think of you,
Shortly will have your freedom.
As anemones that renew
Earth's innocence, be welcome.
Out of your folded sleep
Come, as the western winds come
To pasture with the sheep
On a weary of winter height.
Lie like a pool unwrinkled
That takes the sky to heart,
Where stars and shadows are mingled
And suns run gold with heat.
Return as the winds return,
Heir to an old estate
Of upland, flower and tarn.

But born to essential dark,
To an age that toes the line
And never o'ersteps the mark.
Take off your coat: grow lean:
Suffer humiliation:
Patrol the passes alone,
And eat your iron ration.
Else, wag as the world wags —
One more mechanical jane
Or gentleman in wax.
Is it here we shall regain
Championship? Here awakes
A white hope shall preserve
From flatterers, pimps and fakes
Integrity and nerve?

19

Do not expect again a phœnix hour,
The triple-towered sky, the dove complaining,
Sudden the rain of gold and heart's first ease
Tranced under trees by the eldritch light of sundown.

By a blazed trail our joy will be returning:
One burning hour throws light a thousand ways,
And hot blood stays into familiar gestures.
The best years wait, the body's plenitude.

Consider then, my lover, this is the end
Of the lark's ascending, the hawk's unearthly hover:
Spring season is over soon and first heatwave;
Grave-browed with cloud ponders the huge horizon.

Draw up the dew. Swell with pacific violence.
Take shape in silence. Grow as the clouds grew.
Beautiful brood the cornlands, and you are heavy;
Leafy the boughs — they also hide big fruit.

*   *   *

In this sector when barrage lifts and we
Are left alone with death,
There'll be no time to question strategy.
But now, midsummer offensive not begun,
We wait and draw mutinous breath,
Wondering what to gain
We stake these fallow fields and the good sun.

This has happened to other men before,
Have hung on the lip of danger
And have heard death moving about next door.
Yet I look up at the sky's billowing,
Surprised to find so little change there,
Though in that ample ring
Heaven knows what power lies coiled ready to spring.

What were we at, the moment when we kissed —
Extending the franchise
To an indifferent class, would we enlist
Fresh power who know not how to be so great?
Beget and breed a life — what's this
But to perpetuate
Man's labour, to enlarge a rank estate?

Planted out here some virtue still may flower,
But our dead follies too —
A shock of buried weeds to turn it sour.
Draw up conditions — will the heir conform?
Or thank us for the favour, who
Inherits a bankrupt firm,
Worn-out machinery, an exhausted farm?

* * *

24

Speak then of constancy. Thin eyelids weakly thus
Batted to beauty, lips that reject her, is not this;
Nor lust of eye (Christ said it) denied the final kiss.

Rather a set response, metal-to-magnet affair;
Flows with the tidal blood, like red of rose or fire
Is a fast dye outlasts the fabric of desire.

Happy this river reach sleeps with the sun at noon,
Takes dews and rains to her wide bed, refusing none
That full-filled peace, yet constant to one sea will run.

So melt we down small toys to make each other rich,
Although no getting or spending can extend our reach
Whose poles are love, nor close who closer lie than leech.

For think — throbbing our hearts linked so by endless band,
So geared together, need not otherwise be bound.

*   *   *

26

Beauty breaks ground, oh, in strange places.
Seen after cloudburst down the bone-dry watercourses,
In Texas a great gusher, a grain-
Elevator in the Ukraine plain;
To a new generation turns new faces.

Here too fountains will soon be flowing.
Empty the hills where love was lying late, was playing,
Shall spring to life: we shall find there
Milk and honey for love's heir,
Shadow from sun also, deep ground for growing.

48

My love is a good land. The stranger
Entering here was sure he need prospect no further.
Acres that were the eyes' delight
Now feed another appetite.
What formed her first for seed, for crop must change her.

This is my land. I've overheard it
Making a promise out of clay. All is recorded —
Early green, drought, ripeness, rainfall,
Our village fears and festivals,
When the first tractor came and how we cheered it.

And as the wind whose note will deepen
In the upgrowing tree, who runs for miles to open
His throat above the wood, my song
With that increasing life grew strong,
And will have there a finished form to sleep in.

27

Dropping the few last days, are drops of lead,
Heavier hang than a lifetime on the heart.
Past the limetrees that drug the air jackdaws
Slanting across a sluggish wind go home:
On either side of the Saltway fields of clover
Cling to their sweetness under a threatening sky.
Numb with crisis all, cramped with waiting.
Shallowly breathes the wind or holds his breath,
As in ambush waiting to leap at convoy
Must pass this way — there can be no evasions.
Surly the sky up there and means mischief;
The parchment sky that hourly tightens above us,
Screwed to storm-pitch, where thunder shall roll and roll
Intolerably postponing the last movement.

Now the young challenger, too tired to sidestep,
Hunches to give or take decisive blow.

The climbers from the highest camp set out
Saying goodbye to comrades on the glacier,
A day of rock between them and the summit
That will require their record or their bones.
Now is a charge laid that will split the hill-face,
Tested the wires, the plunger ready to hand.
For time ticks nearer to a rebel hour,
Charging of barricades, bloodshed in city:
The watcher in the window looking out
At the eleventh hour on sun and shadow,
On fixed abodes and the bright air between,
Knows for the first time what he stands to lose.

Crisis afar deadens the nerve, it cools
The blood and hoods imagination's eye,
Whether we apprehend it or remember.
Is fighting on the frontier; little leaks through
Of possible disaster, but one morning
Shells begin to drop in the capital.
So I, indoors for long enough remembering
The round house on the cliff, the springy slopes,
The well in the wood, nor doubting to revisit
But if to see new sunlight on old haunts
Swallows and men come back *but if* come back
From lands *but if* beyond our view *but if*
She dies? Why then, here is a space to let,
The owner gone abroad, never returning.

28

Though bodies are apart
The dark hours so confine
And fuse our hearts, sure, death
Will find no way between.

Narrow this hour, that bed;
But room for us to explore
Pain's long-drawn equator,
The farthest ice of fear.

Storm passes east, recurs:
The beaked lightnings stoop:
The sky falls down: the clouds
Are wrung to the last drop.

Another day is born now.
Woman, your work is done.
This is the end of labour.
Come out into the sun!

*   *   *

From The Magnetic Mountain (1933)

To W. H. Auden

The Magnetic Mountain
Part One

Come, then, companions, this is the spring of blood,
Heart's heyday, movement of masses, beginning of good.
REX WARNER

1

Now to be with you, elate, unshared,
My kestrel joy, O hoverer in wind,
Over the quarry furiously at rest
Chaired on shoulders of shouting wind.

Where's that unique one, wind and wing married,
Aloft in contact of earth and ether;
Feathery my comet, Oh too often
From heaven harried by carrion cares.

No searcher may hope to flush that fleet one
Not to be found by gun or glass,
In old habits, last year's hunting-ground,
Whose beat is wind-wide, whose perch a split second.

But surely will meet him, late or soon,
Who turns a corner into new territory;
Spirit mating afresh shall discern him
On the world's noon-top purely poised.

Void are the valleys, in town no trace,
And dumb the sky-dividing hills:
Swift outrider of lumbering earth
Oh hasten hither my kestrel joy!

2

But Two there are, shadow us everywhere
And will not let us be till we are dead,
Hardening the bones, keeping the spirit spare,
Original in water, earth and air,
Our bitter cordial, our daily bread.

Turning over old follies in ante-room,
For first-born waiting or for late reprieve,
Watching the safety-valve, the slackening loom,
Abed, abroad, at every turn and tomb
A shadow starts, a hand is on your sleeve.

O you, my comrade, now or tomorrow flayed
Alive, crazed by the nibbling nerve; my friend
Whom hate has cornered or whom love betrayed,
By hunger sapped, trapped by a stealthy tide,
Brave for so long but whimpering in the end:

Such are the temporal princes, fear and pain,
Whose borders march with the ice-fields of death,
And from that servitude escape there's none
Till in the grave we set up house alone
And buy our liberty with our last breath.

3

Somewhere beyond the railheads
Of reason, south or north,
Lies a magnetic mountain
Riveting sky to earth.

No line is laid so far.
Ties rusting in a stack
And sleepers — dead men's bones —
Mark a defeated track.

Kestrel who yearly changes
His tenement of space
At the last hovering
May signify that place.

Iron in the soul,
Spirit steeled in fire,
Needle trembling on truth —
These shall draw me there.

The planets keep their course,
Blindly the bee comes home,
And I shall need no sextant
To prove I'm getting warm.

Near that miraculous mountain
Compass and clock must fail,
For space stands on its head there
And time chases its tail.

There's iron for the asking
Will keep all winds at bay,
Girders to take the leaden
Strain of a sagging sky.

Oh there's a mine of metal,
Enough to make me rich
And build right over chaos
A cantilever bridge.

* * *

5

Let us be off! Our steam
Is deafening the dome.
The needle in the gauge

Points to a long-banked rage,
And trembles there to show
What a pressure's below.
Valve cannot vent the strain
Nor iron ribs refrain
That furnace in the heart.
Come on, make haste and start
Coupling-rod and wheel
Welded of patient steel,
Piston that will not stir
Beyond the cylinder
To take in its stride
A teeming countryside.

A countryside that gleams
In the sun's weeping beams;
Where wind-pump, byre and barrow
Are mellowed to mild sorrow,
Agony and sweat
Grown over with regret.
What golden vesper hours
Halo the old grey towers,
What honeyed bells in valleys
Embalm our faiths and follies!
Here are young daffodils
Wind-wanton, and the hills
Have made their peace with heaven.
Oh lovely the heart's haven,
Meadows of endless May,
A spirit's holiday!

Traveller, take care,
Pick no flowers there!

Part Two

Drive your cart and your plough
       over the bones of the dead.
WILLIAM BLAKE

6

Nearing again the legendary isle
Where sirens sang and mariners were skinned,
We wonder now what was there to beguile
That such stout fellows left their bones behind.

Those chorus-girls are surely past their prime,
Voices grow shrill and paint is wearing thin,
Lips that sealed up the sense from gnawing time
Now beg the favour with a graveyard grin.

We have no flesh to spare and they can't bite,
Hunger and sweat have stripped us to the bone;
A skeleton crew we toil upon the tide
And mock the theme-song meant to lure us on:

No need to stop the ears, avert the eyes
From purple rhetoric of evening skies.

7

First Defendant speaks
I that was two am one,
We that were one are two.
Warm in my walled garden the flower grew first,

Transplanted it ran wild on the estate.
Why should it ever need a new sun?
Not navel-string in the cold dawn cut,
Nor a weaned appetite, nor going to school
That autumn did it. Simply, one day
He crossed the frontier and I did not follow:
Returning, spoke another language.
Blessed are they that mourn,
That shear the spring grass from an early grave:
They are not losers, never have known the hour
When an indifferent exile
Passes through the metropolis *en route*
For Newfoundland.

    Mother earth, understand me. You send up
So many leaves to meet the light,
So many flights of birds,
That keep you all their days in shade and song;
And the blown leaf is part of you again
And the frozen blackbird falls into your breast.
Shall not the life-giver be life-receiver?
Am I alone to stand
Outside the natural economy?
Pasteurize mother's milk,
Spoon out the waters of comfort in kilogrammes,
Let love be clinic, let creation's pulse
Keep Greenwich time, guard creature
Against creator, and breed your supermen!
But not from me: for I
Must have life unconditional, or none.
So, like a willow, all its wood curtailed,
I stand by the last ditch of narrowing world,
And stir not, though I see
Pit-heads encroach or glacier crawl down.

      *   *   *

Second Defendant speaks
Let us now praise famous men,
Not your earth-shakers, not the dynamiters,
But who in the Home Counties or the Khyber,
Trimming their nails to meet an ill wind,
Facing the Adversary with a clean collar,
Justified the system.
Admire the venerable pile that bred them,
Bones are its foundations,
The pinnacles are stone abstractions,
Whose halls are whispering-galleries designed
To echo voices of the past, dead tongues.
White hopes of England here
Are taught to rule by learning to obey,
Bend over before vested interests,
Kiss the rod, salute the quarter-deck;
Here is no savage discipline
Of peregrine swooping, of fire destroying,
But a civil code; no capital offender
But the cool cad, the man who goes too far.
Ours the curriculum
Neither of building birds nor wasteful waters,
Bound in book not violent in vein:
Here we inoculate with dead ideas
Against blood-epidemics, against
The infection of faith and the excess of life.
Our methods are up to date; we teach
Through head and not by heart,
Language with gramophones and sex with charts,
Prophecy by deduction, prayer by numbers.
For honours see prospectus: those who leave us
Will get a post and pity the poor;
Their eyes glaze at strangeness;
They are never embarrassed, have a word for everything,
Living on credit, dying when the heart stops;
Will wear black armlets and stand a moment in silence
For the passing of an era, at their own funeral.

11

Third Defendant speaks
I have always acted for the best.
My business is the soul: I have given it rope,
Coaxed it heavenward, but would not let it escape me.
The peoples have sought a Ruler:
I conjured one for each after his own image;
For savage a Dark Demon, for Hebrew a Patriot,
For Christian a Comforter, for atheist a Myth.
The rulers have sought an Ally:
I have called down thunders on the side of authority,
Lightnings to galvanize the law;
Promising the bread of heaven to the hungry of earth,
Shunting the spirit into grassy sidings,
I have served the temporal princes.
There have been men ere now, disturbers of the peace,
Leaders out of my land of milk and honey,
Prescribing harder diet;
Whom I thrashed, outlawed, slew, or if persisting
Deified, shelving them and their dynamite doctrines
Up in the clouds out of the reach of children.
I have always acted for the best:
Hung on the skirts of progress, the tail of revolution,
Ready to drug the defeated and bless the victor.
I am a man apart
Who sits in the dark professing a revelation:
Exploiting the Word with the letter I turn
Joy into sacraments, the Holy Ghost to a formula.
But an impious generation is here,
Let in the light, melt down my mysteries,
Commission the moon to serve my altars
And make my colleagues village entertainers.
That tree of Grace, for years I have tended,
Is a slow-grower, not to be transplanted,
They'll cut it down for pit-props;

That harvest of Faith, not without blood ripened,
They have ploughed in; their dynamos chant
Canticles of a new power: my holy land is blasted,
The crust crumbles, the veins run vinegar.

12

Oh subterranean fires, break out!
Tornadoes, pity not
The petty bourgeois of the soul,
The middleman of God!

Who ruins farm and factory
To keep a private mansion
Is a bad landlord, he shall get
No honourable mention.

Who mobbed the kestrel out of the air,
Who made the tiger tame,
Who lost the blood's inheritance
And found the body's shame;

Who raised his hands to brand a Cain
And bless a submarine —
Time is up: the medicine-man
Must take his medicine.

The winter evening holds her peace
And makes a crystal pause;
Frozen are all the streams of light,
Silent about their source.

Comrade, let us look to earth,
Be stubborn, act and sleep:
Here at our feet the lasting skull
Keeps a stiff upper lip:

Feeling the weight of a long winter,
Grimaces underground;
But never again will need to ask
Why spirit was flesh-bound.

And we whom winter days oppress
May find some work to hand,
Perfect our plans, renew parts,
Break hedges down, plough land.

So when primroses pave the way
And the sun warms the stone,
We may receive the exile spirit
Coming into its own.

13

Fourth Defendant speaks
To sit at head of one's own table,
To overlook a warm familiar landscape,
Have large cupboards for small responsibilities —
Surely that does outweigh
The rent veil and the agonies to follow?
Me the Almighty fixed, from Eve fallen,
Heart-deep in earth, a pointer to star fields,
Suffering sapflow, fruitage, early barrenness;
Changeable reputed, but to change constant,
Fickle of fashion no more than the months are;
Daily depend on surroundings for sustenance,
On what my roots reach, what my leaves inhale here.
Grant me a rich ground, wrapped in airs temperate,
Not where nor'-easters threaten the flint scarps;
Consequence then shall I have, men's admiration
Now, and my bones shall be fuel for the future.
Yet have I always failed.
For he, who should have been my prime possession,
Was not to be possessed.

I leant o'er him, a firmament of shadow,
But he looked up through me and saw the stars.
I would have bound him in the earth-ways,
Fluid, immediate, the child of nature.
But he made bricks of earth, iron from fire,
Turned waves to power, winds to communication;
Setting up Art against Chaos, subjecting
My flux to the synthetic frost of reason.
I am left with a prone man,
Virtue gone out of him; who in the morning
Will rise to join Crusades or assist the Harlequins.
Though I persuade him that his stars are mine eyes'
Refraction, that wisdom's best expressed in
The passive mood, — here's no change for the better:
I was the body's slave, am now the spirit's.
Come, let me contemplate my own
Mysteries, a dark glass may save my face.

14

Live you by love confined,
There is no nearer nearness;
Break not his light bounds,
The stars' and seas' harness:
There is nothing beyond,
We have found the land's end.
We'll take no mortal wound
Who felt him in the furnace,
Drowned in his fierceness,
By his midsummer browned:
Nor ever lose awareness
Of nearness and farness
Who've stood at earth's heart careless
Of suns and storms around,
Who have leant on the hedge of the wind,
On the last ledge of darkness.

We are where love has come
To live: he is that river
Which flows and is the same;
He is not the famous deceiver
Nor early-flowering dream.
Content you. Be at home
In me. There's but one room
Of all the house you may never
Share, deny or enter.
There, as a candle's beam
Stands firm and will not waver
Spire-straight in a close chamber,
As though in shadowy cave a
Stalagmite of flame,
The integral spirit climbs
The dark in light for ever.

15

Consider. These are they
Who have a stake in earth
But risk no wing on air,
Walk not a planet path.

Theirs the reward of all
That live by sap alone,
Flourishing but to show
Which way the wind has gone.

While oaks of pedigree
Stand over a rich seam,
Another sinks the shaft,
Fills furnace, gets up steam.

These never would break through
The orbit of their year,
Admit no altered stress,
Decline a change of gear.

The tree grips soil, the bird
Knows how to use the wind;
But the full man must live
Rooted yet unconfined.

Part Three

Never yield before the barren.
D.H. LAWRENCE

* * *

18

Not hate nor love, but say
Refreshment after rain,
A lucid hour; though this
Need not occur again.

You shall no further feast
Your pride upon my flesh.
Cry for the moon: here's but
An instantaneous flash.

My wells, my rooted good
Go deeper than you dare:
Seek not my sun and moon,
They are centred elsewhere.

I know a fairer land,
Whose furrows are of fire,
Whose hills are a pure metal
Shining for all to share.

And there all rivers run
To magnify the sea,
Whose waves recur for ever
In calm equality.

Hands off! The dykes are down.
This is no time for play.
Hammer is poised and sickle
Sharpened. I cannot stay.

*   *   *

23

Fourth Enemy speaks
I'm a dreamer, so are you.
See the pink sierras call,
The ever-ever land of dew,
Magic basements, fairy coal.
There the youngest son wins through,
Wee Willie can thrash the bully,
Living's cheap and dreams come true;
Lying manna tempts the belly;
Crowns are many, claims are few.

Come along then, come away
From the rush hour, from the town:
Blear and overcast today
Would put a blackcap out of tune,
Spoil the peacock's June display.

Rigid time of driving-belts
Gives no rest for grace-notes gay:
Fear and fever, cables, bolts
Pin the soul, allow no play.

You're a poet, so am I:
No man's keeper, intimate
Of breeding earth and brooding sky,
Irresponsible, remote,
A cool cloud, creation's eye.
Seek not to turn the winter tide
But to temperate deserts fly:
Close chain-mail of solitude
Must protect you or you die.

Come away then, let us go;
Lose identity and pass
Through the still blockade of snow,
Fear's frontier, an age of ice:
Pierce the crust and pass below
Towards a red volcanic core,
The warm womb where flesh can grow
Again and passion sleep secure
In creative ebb and flow.

24

Tempt me no more; for I
Have known the lightning's hour,
The poet's inward pride,
The certainty of power.

Bayonets are closing round.
I shrink; yet I must wring
A living from despair
And out of steel a song.

Though song, though breath be short,
I'll share not the disgrace
Of those that ran away
Or never left the base.

Comrades, my tongue can speak
No comfortable words,
Calls to a forlorn hope,
Gives work and not rewards.

Oh keep the sickle sharp
And follow still the plough:
Others may reap, though some
See not the winter through.

Father, who endest all,
Pity our broken sleep;
For we lie down with tears
And waken but to weep.

And if our blood alone
Will melt this iron earth,
Take it. It is well spent
Easing a saviour's birth.

25

Consider these, for we have condemned them;
Leaders to no sure land, guides their bearings lost
Or in league with robbers have reversed the signposts,
Disrespectful to ancestors, irresponsible to heirs.
Born barren, a freak growth, root in rubble,
Fruitlessly blossoming, whose foliage suffocates,
Their sap is sluggish, they reject the sun.

The man with his tongue in his cheek, the woman
With her heart in the wrong place, unhandsome, unwholesome;

69

Have exposed the new-born to worse than weather,
Exiled the honest and sacked the seer.
These drowned the farms to form a pleasure-lake,
In time of drought they drain the reservoir
Through private pipes for baths and sprinklers.

Getters not begetters; gainers not beginners;
Whiners, no winners; no triers, betrayers;
Who steer by no star, whose moon means nothing.
Daily denying, unable to dig:
At bay in villas from blood relations,
Counters of spoons and content with cushions
They pray for peace, they hand down disaster.

They that take the bribe shall perish by the bribe,
Dying of dry rot, ending in asylums,
A curse to children, a charge on the state.
But still their fears and frenzies infect us;
Drug nor isolation will cure this cancer:
It is now or never, the hour of the knife,
The break with the past, the major operation.

Part Four

He comes with work to do, he does not come to coo.
GERARD MANLEY HOPKINS

26

Junction or terminus — here we alight.
A myriad tracks converge on this moment,
This man where all ages and men are married,
Who shall right him? Who shall determine?

Standing astonished at the close of day
We know the worst, we may guess at good:
Geared too high our power was wasted,
Who have lost the old way to the happy ending.

A world behind us the west is in flames,
Devastated areas, works at a standstill;
No seed awakes, wary is no hunter,
The tame are ruined and the wild have fled.

Where then the saviour, the stop of illness?
Hidden the mountain was to steel our hearts.
Is healing here? An untrodden territory
Promises no coolness, invites but the brave.

But see! Not far, not fiction, a real one,
Vibrates like heat-haze full in the sun's face
Filling the heart, that chaste and fleet one,
Rarely my kestrel, my lucky star.

O man perplexed, here is your answer.
Alone who soars, who feeds upon earth —
Him shall you heed and learn where joy is
The dance of action, the expert eye.

Now is your moment, O hang-fire heart;
The ice is breaking, the death-grip relaxes,
Luck's turned. Submit to your star and take
Command, Oh start the attacking movement!

*   *   *

28

Though winter's barricade delays,
Another season's in the air;
We'll sow the spring in our young days,
Found a Virginia everywhere.

Look where the ranks of crocuses
Their rebel colours will display
Coming with quick fire to redress
The balance of a wintry day.

Those daffodils that from the mould
Drawing a sweet breath soon shall flower,
With a year's labour get their gold
To spend it on a sunny hour.

They from earth's centre take their time
And from the sun what love they need:
The proud flower burns away its prime,
Eternity lies in the seed.

Follow the kestrel, south or north,
Strict eye, spontaneous wing can tell
A secret. Where he comes to earth
Is the heart's treasure. Mark it well.

Here he hovers. You're on the scent;
Magnetic mountain is not far,
Across no gulf or continent,
Not where you think but where you are.

Stake out your claim. Go downwards. Bore
Through the tough crust. Oh learn to feel
A way in darkness to good ore.
You are the magnet and the steel.

Out of that dark a new world flowers.
There in the womb, in the rich veins
Are tools, dynamos, bridges, towers,
Your tractors and your travelling-cranes.

29

But winter still rides rough-shod upon us,
Summer comes not for wishing nor warmth at will:
Passes are blocked and glaciers pen us
Round the hearth huddled, hoping for a break,
Playing at patience, reporting ill.
Aware of changed temperature one shall wake
And rushing to window arouse companions
To feel frost surrender, an ice age finished;
Whose strength shall melt from the mountains and run
Riot, careering down corries and canyons.
What floods will rise then through rivers replenished,
Embankments broken, and bluffs undone,
Laid low old follies, all landmarks vanished.
Is it ready for launching, the Argo, the Ark,
Our transport, our buoyant one, our heart of oak?

Make haste, put through the emergency order
For an overtime day, for double shifts working:
Weather is breaking, tomorrow we must board her,
Cast off onto chaos and shape a course.
Many months have gone to her making,
Wood well-seasoned for watertight doors,
The old world's best in her ribs and ballast,
White-heat, high pressure, the heart of a new
In boiler, in gadget, in gauge, in screw.
Peerless on water, Oh proud our palace,
A home for heroes, the latest of her line;
A beater to windward, obedient to rudder,
A steamer into storm, a hurricane-rider,
Foam-stepper, star-steerer, freighter and fighter —
Name her, release her, anoint her with wine!

Whom shall we take with us? The true, the tested,
Floods over to find a new world and man it,
Sure-foot, Surveyor, Spark and Strong,

Those whom winter has wasted, not worsted,
Good at their jobs for a break-down gang:
Born haters will blast through debris or granite,
Willing work on the permanent ways,
And natural lovers repair the race.
As needle to north, as wheel in wheel turning,
Men shall know their masters and women their need,
Mating and submitting, not dividing and defying,
Force shall fertilize, mass shall breed.
Broad let our valleys embrace the morning
And satisfied see a good day dying,
Accepting the shadows, sure of seed.

30

You who would come with us,
Think what you stand to lose —
An assured income, the will
In your favour and the feel
Of firmness underfoot.
For travellers by this boat
Nothing to rest the eyes on
But a migrant's horizon,
No fixtures or bric-a-brac —
Wave walls without a break.
Old acquaintance on the quay
Have come to clutch your knee —
Merry-Andrew and Cassandra,
Squeamish, Sponge and Squanderer,
The Insurance Agent, the Vicar,
Hard Cheese the Confidence-Tricker,
Private Loot, General Pride,
And Lust the sultry-eyed.
Others you hate to leave
Wave with autumnal grief,

The best of what has been,
Props of an English scene;
A day we may not recover,
A camp you must quit for ever.

Now, if you will, retract.
For we are off to act
Activity of young
And cut the ravelled string.
Calm yourselves, you that seek
The flame, and whose flesh is weak
Must keep it in cold storage:
For we shall not encourage
The would-be hero, the nervous
Martyr to rule or serve us.
Stand forward for volunteers
Who have tempered their loves and fears
In the skilled process of time,
Whose spirit is blown to a flame
That leaves no mean alloys.
You who have heard a voice —
The siren in the morning
That gives the worker warning,
The whisper from the loam
Promising life to come,
Manifesto of peace
Read in an altered face —
Who have heard; and believe it true
That new life must break through.

31

In happier times
When the heart is whole and the exile king returned
We may sing shock of opposing teams
And electric storms of love again.

Our voices may be tuned
To solo flight, to record-breaking plane;
Looking down from hill
We may follow with fresh felicities
Wilful the light, the wayward motion of trees,
In happier times when the heart is whole.

In happier times
When the land is ours, these springs shall irrigate
Good growing soil until it teems,
Redeemed from mortgage, drilled to obey;
But still must flow in spate.
We'll focus stars again; though now must be
Map and binoculars
Outlining vision, bringing close
Natural features that will need no glass
In happier times, when the land is ours.

Make us a wind
To shake the world out of this sleepy sickness
Where flesh has dwindled and brightness waned!
New life multiple in seed and cell
Mounts up to brace our slackness.
Oppression's passion, a full organ swell
Through our throats welling wild
Of angers in unison arise
And hunger haunted with a million sighs,
Make us a wind to shake the world!

Make us the wind
From a new world that springs and gathers force,
Clearing the air, cleaning the wound;
Sets masses in motion and whips the blood.
Oh they shall find him fierce
Who cling to relics, dead wood shall feel his blade.
Rudely the last leaves whirled,
A storm on fire, dry ghosts, shall go in
Fear and be laid in the red of their own ruin.
Make us the wind from a new world!

You that love England, who have an ear for her music,
The slow movement of clouds in benediction,
Clear arias of light thrilling over her uplands,
Over the chords of summer sustained peacefully;
Ceaseless the leaves' counterpoint in a west wind lively,
Blossom and river rippling loveliest allegro,
And the storms of wood strings brass at year's finale:
Listen. Can you not hear the entrance of a new theme?

You who go out alone, on tandem or on pillion,
Down arterial roads riding in April,
Or sad beside lakes where hill-slopes are reflected
Making fires of leaves, your high hopes fallen:
Cyclists and hikers in company, day excursionists,
Refugees from cursed towns and devastated areas;
Know you seek a new world, a saviour to establish
Long-lost kinship and restore the blood's fulfilment.

You who like peace, good sorts, happy in a small way
Watching birds or playing cricket with schoolboys,
Who pay for drinks all round, whom disaster chose not;
Yet passing derelict mills and barns roof-rent
Where despair has burnt itself out — hearts at a standstill,
Who suffer loss, aware of lowered vitality;
We can tell you a secret, offer a tonic; only
Submit to the visiting angel, the strange new healer.

You above all who have come to the far end, victims
Of a run-down machine, who can bear it no longer;
Whether in easy chairs chafing at impotence
Or against hunger, bullies and spies preserving
The nerve for action, the spark of indignation —
Need fight in the dark no more, you know your enemies.
You shall be leaders when zero hour is signalled,
Wielders of power and welders of a new world.

*　*　*

(for Frances Warner)

What do we ask for, then?
Not for pity's pence nor pursy affluence,
Only to set up house again:
Neither a coward's heaven, cessation of pain,
Nor a new world of sense,
But that we may be given the chance to be men.
For what, then, do we hope?
Not longer sight at once but enlarged scope;
Miraculous no seed or growth of soul, but soil
Cleared of weed, prepared for good:
We shall expect no birth-hour without blood
Nor fire without recoil.

Publish the vision, broadcast and screen it,
Of a world where the will of all shall be raised-to highest
     power,
Village or factory shall form the unit.
Control shall be from the centres, quick brain, warm heart,
And the bearings bathed in a pure
Fluid of sympathy. There possessions no more shall be part
Of the man, where riches and sacrifice
Are of flesh and blood, sex, muscles, limbs and eyes.
Each shall give of his best. It shall seem proper
For all to share what all produced.
Men shall be glad of company, love shall be more than a
     guest
And the bond no more of paper.

Open your eyes, for vision
Is here of a world that has ceased to be bought and sold
With traitor silver and fairy gold;
But the diamond of endurance, the wrought-iron of passion
Is all their currency.
As the body that knows through action they are splendid,
Feeling head and heart agree;

Young men proud of their output, women no longer stale
With deferred crisis; the old, a full day ended,
Able to stand down and sit still.
Only the exploiter, the public nuisance, the quitter
Receive no quarter.

Here they do not need
To flee the birthplace. There's room for growing and working.
Bright of eye, champions for speed,
They sing their own songs, they are active, they play not
      watch:
Happy at night talking
Of the demon bowler cracked over the elm-trees,
The reverse pass that won the match.
At festivals knowing themselves normal and well-born
They remember the ancestors that gave them ease,
Harris who fought the bully at Melbourne,
What Wainwright wrote with his blood, Rosa in prison —
All who sucked out the poison.

35

In these our winter days
Death's iron tongue is glib
Numbing with fear all flesh upon
A fiery-hearted globe.

An age once green is buried,
Numbered the hours of light;
Blood-red across the snow our sun
Still trails his faint retreat.

Spring through death's iron guard
Her million blades shall thrust;
Love that was sleeping, not extinct,
Throw off the nightmare crust.

Eyes, though not ours, shall see
Sky-high a signal flame,
The sun returned to power above
A world, but not the same.

36

Now raise your voices for a final chorus,
Lift the glasses, drink tomorrow's health —
Success to the doctor who is going to cure us
And those who will die no more in bearing wealth.
On our magnetic mountain a beacon burning
Shall sign the peace we hoped for, soon or late,
Clear over a clean earth, and all men turning
Like infants' eyes like sunflowers to the light.

Drink to the ordered nerves, the sight restored;
A day when power for all shall radiate
From the sovereign centres, and the blood is stirred
To flow in its ancient courses of love and hate:
When the country vision is ours that like a barn
Fills the heart with slow-matured delight,
Absorbing wind and summer, till we turn
Like infants' eyes like sunflowers to the light.

For us to dream the birthday, but they shall act it —
Bells over fields, the hooters from the mine,
On New Year's Eve under the bridegroom's attic
Chorus of coastguards singing Auld Lang Syne.
Now at hope's horizon that day is dawning,
We guess at glory from a mountain height,
But then in valley towns they will be turning
Like infants' eyes like sunflowers to the light.

Beckon O beacon, and O sun be soon!
Hollo, bells, over a melting earth!
Let man be many and his sons all sane,
Fearless with fellows, handsome by the hearth.
Break from your trance: start dancing now in town,
And, fences down, the ploughing match with mate.
This is your day: so turn, my comrades, turn
Like infants' eyes like sunflowers to the light.

From A Time to Dance (1935)

Learning to Talk

See this small one, tiptoe on
The green foothills of the years,
Views a younger world than yours;
When you go down, he'll be the tall one.

Dawn's dew is on his tongue —
No word for what's behind the sky,
Naming all that meets the eye,
Pleased with sunlight over a lawn.

Hear his laughter. He can't contain
The exquisite moment overflowing.
Limbs leaping, woodpecker flying
Are for him and not hereafter.

Tongue trips, recovers, triumphs,
Turning all ways to express
What the forward eye can guess —
That time is his and earth young.

We are growing too like trees
To give the rising wind a voice:
Eagles shall build upon our verse,
Our winged seeds are tomorrow's sowing.

Yes, we learn to speak for all
Whose hearts here are not at home,
All who march to a better time
And breed the world for which they burn.

Though we fall once, though we often,
Though we fall to rise not again,
From our horizon sons begin;
When we go down, they will be tall ones.

The Conflict

I sang as one
Who on a tilting deck sings
To keep men's courage up, though the wave hangs
That shall cut off their sun.

As storm-cocks sing,
Flinging their natural answer in the wind's teeth,
And care not if it is waste of breath
Or birth-carol of spring.

As ocean-flyer clings
To height, to the last drop of spirit driving on
While yet ahead is land to be won
And work for wings.

Singing I was at peace,
Above the clouds, outside the ring:
For sorrow finds a swift release in song
And pride its poise.

Yet living here,
As one between two massing powers I live
Whom neutrality cannot save
Nor occupation cheer.

None such shall be left alive:
The innocent wing is soon shot down,
And private stars fade in the blood-red dawn
Where two worlds strive.

The red advance of life
Contracts pride, calls out the common blood,
Beats song into a single blade,
Makes a depth-charge of grief.

Move then with new desires,
For where we used to build and love
Is no man's land, and only ghosts can live
Between two fires.

Losers

Those are judged losers and fortune-flouted
Whose flighted hopes fell down short of satisfaction;
The killed in action, the blasted in beauty, all choosers

Of the wrong channel for love's seasonal spate:
Cheerless some amid rock or rank forest life-long
Laboured to hew an estate, but they died childless:

Those within hail of home by blizzard o'ertaken;
Those awakening from vision with truth on tongue, struck
    dumb:
Are deemed yet to have been transfigured in failure.

Men mourn their beauty and promise, publish the diaries;
Medals are given; the graves are evergreen with pity:
Their fire is forwarded through the hearts of the living.

What can we say of these, from the womb wasted,
Whose nerve was never tested in act, who fell at the start,
Who had no beauty to lose, born out of season?

Early an iron frost clamped down their flowing
Desires. They were lost at once: they failed and died in the
     whirling
Snow, bewildered, homeless from first to last.

Frightened we stop our ears to the truth they are telling
Who toil to remain alive, whose children start from sleep
Weeping into a world worse than nightmares.

Splendour of cities they built cannot ennoble
The barely living, ambitious for bread alone. Pity
Trails not her robe for these and their despairs.

In Me Two Worlds

In me two worlds at war
Trample the patient flesh,
This lighted ring of sense where clinch
Heir and ancestor.

This moving point of dust
Where past and future meet
Traces their battle-line and shows
Each thrust and counterthrust.

The armies of the dead
Are trenched within my bones,
My blood's their semaphore, their wings
Are watchers overhead.

Their captains stand at ease
As on familiar ground,
The veteran longings of the heart
Serve them for mercenaries.

Conscious of power and pride
Imperially they move
To pacify an unsettled zone —
The life for which they died.

But see, from vision's height
March down the men to come,
And in my body rebel cells
Look forward to the fight.

The insolence of the dead
Breaks on their solid front:
They tap my nerves for power, my veins
To stain their banners red.

These have the spirit's range,
The measure of the mind:
Out of the dawn their fire comes fast
To conquer and to change.

So heir and ancestor
Pursue the inveterate feud,
Making my senses' darkened fields
A theatre of war.

Sonnet

This man was strong, and like a seacape parted
The tides. There were not continents enough
For all his fledged ambitions. The hard-hearted
Mountains were moved by his explosive love.

Was young: yet between island and island
Laid living cable and whispered across seas:
When he sang, our feathery woods fell silent:
His smile put the fidgeting hours at ease.

See him now, a cliff chalk-faced and crumbling,
Eyes like craters of volcanoes dead;
A miser with the tarnished minutes fumbling,
A queasy traveller from board to bed:
The voice that charmed spirits grown insane
As the barking of dogs at the end of a dark lane.

Two Songs

1

I've heard them lilting at loom and belting,
Lasses lilting before dawn of day:
But now they are silent, not gamesome and gallant —
The flowers of the town are rotting away.

There was laughter and loving in the lanes at evening;
Handsome were the boys then, and girls were gay.
But lost in Flanders by medalled commanders
The lads of the village are vanished away.

Cursed be the promise that takes our men from us —
All will be champion if you choose to obey:
They fight against hunger but still it is stronger —
The prime of our land grows cold as the clay.

The women are weary, once lilted so merry,
Waiting to marry for a year and a day:
From wooing and winning, from owning or earning
The flowers of the town are all turned away.

Come, live with me and be my love,
And we will all the pleasures prove
Of peace and plenty, bed and board,
That chance employment may afford.

I'll handle dainties on the docks
And thou shalt read of summer frocks:
At evening by the sour canals
We'll hope to hear some madrigals.

Care on thy maiden brow shall put
A wreath of wrinkles, and thy foot
Be shod with pain: not silken dress
But toil shall tire thy loveliness.

Hunger shall make thy modest zone
And cheat fond death of all but bone —
If these delights thy mind may move,
Then live with me and be my love.

A Carol

Oh hush thee, my baby,
Thy cradle's in pawn:
No blankets to cover thee
Cold and forlorn.
The stars in the bright sky
Look down and are dumb
At the heir of the ages
Asleep in a slum.

The hooters are blowing,
No heed let him take;
When baby is hungry
'Tis best not to wake.

Thy mother is crying,
Thy dad's on the dole:
Two shillings a week is
The price of a soul.

A Time to Dance

In memory of L.P. Hedges

For those who had the power
    of the forest fires that burn
Leaving their source in ashes
    to flush the sky with fire:
Those whom a famous urn
    could not contain, whose passion
Brimmed over the deep grave
    and dazzled epitaphs:
For all that have won us wings
    to clear the tops of grief,
My friend who within me laughs
    bids you dance and sing.

Some set out to explore
    earth's limit, and little they recked if
Never their feet came near it
    outgrowing the need for glory:
Some aimed at a small objective
    but the fierce updraught of their spirit
Forced them to the stars.
    Are honoured in public who built
The dam that tamed a river;
    or holding the salient for hours
Against odds, cut off and killed,
    are remembered by one survivor.

All these. But most for those
    whom accident made great,
As a radiant chance encounter
    of cloud and sunlight grows
Immortal on the heart:
    whose gift was the sudden bounty
Of a passing moment, enriches
    the fulfilled eye for ever.
Their spirits float serene
    above time's roughest reaches,
But their seed is in us and over
    our lives they are evergreen.

*   *   *

Let us sing then for my friend not a dirge, not a funeral
    anthem,
But words to match his mirth, a theme with a happy end;
A bird's buoyancy in them, over the dark-toned earth
To hold a sustained flight, a tune sets death to dancing;
The stormcock's song, the ecstatic poise of the natural
    fighter,
And a beat as of feet advancing to glory, a lilt emphatic.

*   *   *

In February, a world of hard light,
A frosty welcome, the aconites came up
Lifting their loving cups to drink the sun:
Spring they meant, mounting and more of hope.
And I thought of my friend, like these withered too soon,
Who went away in a night
Before the spring was ready, who left our town
For good. Like aconites he pledged the spring
Out of my grief-bound heart, and he made me sing
The spirit of life that nothing can keep down.

But yesterday, in May, a storm arose
Clouding the spring's festivities, and spoilt
Much would have been admired and given us shade.
We saw this year's young hopes beat down and soiled,
Blossoms not now for fruit, boughs might have made
Syringa's wreath of snows.
A fortune gone time held for us in trust.
And I knew no bold flourish of flowers can write
Off the dead loss, when friends dissolve in night
Changing our dear-invested love to dust.

Strange ways the dead break through. Not the Last Post
Brings them, nor clanging midnight: for then is the inner
Heart reinforced against assault and sap.
On break-up day or at the cricket-club dinner
Between a word and a word they find the gap,
And we know what we have lost.
Sorrow is natural thirst: we are not weaned
At once. Though long withdrawn the sickening blade,
Deeply we remember loss of blood
And the new skin glosses over an active wound.

Remember that winter morning — no maroon
Warned of a raid; death granted no farewell speech,
Acted without prologue, was a bell and a line
Speaking from far of one no more within reach.
Blood ran out of me. I was alone.
How suddenly, how soon,
In a moment, while I was looking the other way,
You hid yourself where I could never find you —
Too dark the shadows earth sheeted around you.
So we went home: that was the close of play.

Still I hoped for news. Often I stood
On promontories that straining towards the west
Fret their hearts away. Thence on a clear
Day one should glimpse the islands of the blest,
And he, if any, had a passport there.

But no, it was no good.
Those isles, it proved, were broken promises,
A trick of light, a way wishes delude:
Or, if he lived out there, no cable was laid
To carry his love whispering over seas.

So I returned. Perhaps he was nearer home
And I had missed him. Here he was last seen
Walking familiar as sunlight a solid road;
Round the next turn, his door. But look, there has been
Landslide: those streets end abruptly, they lead
The eye into a tomb.
Scrabble for souvenirs. Fit bone to bone;
Anatomy of buried joys you guess,
But the wind jeers through it. Assemble the shattered glass;
A mirror you have, but the face there is your own.

Was so much else we could have better spared —
Churches, museums, multiple stores: but the bomb
Fell on the power-house: total that eclipse.
He was our dynamo, our warmth, our beam
Transmitter of mirth — it is a town's collapse
Not easily repaired.
Or as a reservoir that, sharing out
Rain hoarded from heaven, springs from the valley,
Refreshment was for all: now breached and wholly
Drained, is a barren bed, a cup of drought.

Then to the hills, as one who dies for rain,
I went. All day the light makes lovely passes
There, whose hands are healing, whose smile was yours,
And eloquent winds hearten the dry grasses.
They have come to terms with death: for them the year's
Harvest, the instant pain,
Are as clouds passing indifferent over
Their heads, but certain givers in the end.
Downright these hills, hiding nothing they stand
Firm to the foot and comfort the eye for ever.

They say, 'Death is above your weight, too strong
For argument or armies, the real dictator:
He never was one to answer the question, Why?
He sends for you tomorrow, for us later:
Nor are you that Orpheus who could buy
Resurrection with a song.
Not for long will your chalk-faced bravado
Stand the erosion of eternity:
Learn from us a moment's sanity —
To be warm in the sun, to accept the following shadow.'

In my heart's mourning underworld I sang
As miners entombed singing despair to sleep —
Their earth is stopped, their eyes are reconciled
To night. Yet here, under the sad hill-slope
Where I thought one spring of my life for ever was sealed,
The friend I had lost sprang
To life again and showed me a mystery:
For I knew, at last wholly accepting death,
Though earth had taken his body and air his breath,
He was not in heaven or earth: he was in me.

Now will be cloudburst over a countryside
Where the tongues of prophets were dry and the air was
        aching:
Sky-long the flash, the thunder, the release,
Are fresh beginning, the hour of the weather breaking.
Sing, you watercourses, bringers of peace!
Valleys, open wide
Your cracked lips! You shall be green again
And ease with flowers what the sun has seared.
Waking tomorrow we'll find the air cleared,
Sunny with fresh eloquence after rain.

For my friend that was dead is alive. He bore transplanting
Into a common soil. Strongly he grows
Upon the heart and gives the tentative wing
Take-off for flights, surety for repose.

And he returns not in an echoing
Regret, a hollow haunting,
Not as a shadow thrown across our day;
But radiant energy, charging the mind with power
That all who are wired to receive him surely can share.
It is no flying visit: he comes to stay.

His laughter was better than birds in the morning: his smile
Turned the edge of the wind: his memory
Disarms death and charms the surly grave.
Early he went to bed, too early we
Saw his light put out: yet we could not grieve
More than a little while,
For he lives in the earth around us, laughs from the sky.
Soon he forgave — still generous to a fault —
My crippling debt of sorrow, and I felt
In grief's hard winter earth's first melting sigh.

Think. One breath of midsummer will start
A buried life — on sunday boys content
Hearing through study windows a gramophone,
Sweet peas arrested on a morning scent —
And the man sighs for what he has outgrown.
He wastes pity. The heart
Has all recorded. Each quaver of distress,
Mirth's every crotchet, love's least tremolo —
Scarce-noted notes that to full movements flow —
Have made their mark on its deep tenderness.

Much more should he, who had life and to spare,
Be here impressed, his sympathy relayed
Out of the rich-toned past. And is. For through
Desert my heart he gives a fiery lead,
Unfolding contours, lengthening the view.
He is a thoroughfare
Over all sliding sands. Each stopping-place
Wears his look of welcome. May even find,
When I come to the snow-line, the bitter end,
His hand-holds cut on death's terrific face.

Distant all that, and heaven a hearsay word —
Truth's fan-vaulting, vision carved in flight
Perhaps, or the last delirium of self-loving.
But now a word in season, a dance in spite
Of death: love, the affirmative in all living,
Blossom, dew or bird.
For one is dead, but his love has gone before
Us, pointing and paving a way into the future;
Has gone to form its very flesh and feature,
The air we shall breathe, the kindling for our fire.

Nothing is lost. There is a thrifty wife,
Conceives all, saves all, finds a use for all.
No waste her deserts: limited rock, lightnings
And speedwell that run riot, seas that spill
Over, grass and man — whatever springs
From her excess of life
Is active and passive, spending and receipt.
And he took after her, a favourite son
In whom she excelled, through whom were handed on
Dewy her morning and her lasting heat.

Now we have sorrow's range, no more delaying —
Let the masked batteries of spring flash out
From ridge and copse, and flowers like shrapnel burst
Along the lanes, and all her land-mines spout
Quick and hanging green. Our best, our boast,
Our mood and month of maying,
For winter's bleak blockade is broken through
And every street flies colours of renaissance.
Today the hawk goes up for reconnaissance,
The heart beats faster having earth's ends in view.

Leave to the mercies of the manifold grass,
Will cover all earth's faults, what in his clay
Were but outcrops of volcanic life.
You shall recall one open as the day,
Many-mooded as the light above

English hills where pass
Sunlight and storm to a large reconciling.
You shall recall how it was warmth to be
With him — a feast, a first of June; that he
Was generous, that he attacked the bowling.

Lay laurels here, and leave your tears to dry —
Sirs, his last wishes were that you should laugh.
For those in whom was found life's richest seam
Yet they asked no royalty, one cenotaph
Were thanks enough — a world where none may scheme
To hoard, while many die,
Life; where all lives grow from an equal chance.
Tomorrow we resume building: but this
Day he calls holiday, he says it is
A time to dance, he calls you all to dance.

Today the land that knew him shall do him honour,
Sun be a spendthrift, fields come out with gold,
Severn and Windrush be Madrigal and Flowing,
Woodlarks flash up like rockets and unfold
In showers of song, cloud-shadows pace the flying
Wind, the champion runner.
Joy has a flying start, our hopes like flames
Lengthen their stride over a kindled earth,
And noon cheers all, upstanding in the south.
Sirs, be merry: these are his funeral games.

From Noah and the Waters (1936)

To Charles Fenby

Second Chorus

Since you have come thus far,
Your visible past a steamer's wake continually fading
Among the receding hours tumbled, and yet you carry
Souvenirs of dead ports, a freight of passion and fear,
Remembrance of loves and landfalls and much deep-sea
    predicament
Active upon the heart: — consider by what star
Your reckoning is, and whether conscious a course you steer
Or whether you rudderless yaw, self-mutinied, all at sea.

You have come far
To the brink of this tableland where the next step treads air,
Your thoughts like antennæ feeling doubtfully towards the
    future,
Your will swerving all ways to evade that unstable void;
High stakes, hard falls, comfortless contacts lie before,
But to sidestep these is to die upon a waterless plateau;
You must uncase and fly, for ahead is your thoroughfare.

Consider Noah's fate,
Chosen to choose between two claims irreconcilable,
Alive on this island, old friends at his elbow, the floods at
    his feet.
Whether the final sleep, fingers curled about
The hollow comfort of a day worn smooth as holy relics;
Or trusting to walk the waters, to see when they abate
A future solid for sons and for him the annealing rainbow.

It is your fate
Also to choose. On the one hand all that habit endears:
The lawn is where bishops have walked; the walled garden is
    private
Though your bindweed lust overruns it; the roses are sweet
    dying;

Soil so familiar to your roots you cannot feel it effete.
On the other hand what dearth engenders and what death
Makes flourish: the need and dignity of bearing fruit, the
    fight
For resurrection, the exquisite grafting on stranger stock.

   Stand with us here and now
Consider the force of these waters, the mobile face of the
    flood
Trusting and terrible as a giant who turns from sleep. Think
    how
You called them symbols of purity and yet you daily defiled
    them:
They failed you never; for that they were always the
    disregarded.
Ubiquitous to your need they made the barley grow
Or bore you to new homes; they kept you hale and
    handsome.
Of all flesh they were the sign and substance. All things flow.

   Stand with us now
Looking back on a time you have spent, a land that you
    know.
Ask what formed the dew and dressed the evening in awe;
What hands made buoyant your ships, what shaped the
    impatient prow,
Turned sea-shells and dynamos and wheels on river and
    railroad:
Truth's bed and earth's refreshment — one everywhere
    element
In the tissue of man, the tears of his anger, the sweat of his
    brow.

   Then look with Noah's eyes
On the waters that wait his choice. Not only are they
    insurgent
Over the banks and shallows of their birthplace, but they
    rise

Also in Noah's heart: their rippling fingers erase
The ill-favoured façade of his present, the weird ancestral
    folly,
The maze of mirrors, the corrupting admirers, the silted lies.
Now must he lay his naked virtue upon their knees.

  Then turn your eyes
Upon that unbounded prospect and your dwindling island of
    ease,
Measuring your virtue against its challenger, measuring well
Your leap across the gulf, as the swallow-flock that flies
In autumn gathers its strength on some far-sighted headland.
Learn the migrant's trust, the intuition of longer
Sunlight: be certain as they you have only winter to lose,
And believe that beyond this flood a kinder country lies.

From Overtures to Death (1938)

To E. M. Forster

Maple and Sumach

Maple and sumach down this autumn ride —
Look, in what scarlet character they speak!
For this their russet and rejoicing week
Trees spend a year of sunsets on their pride.
You leaves drenched with the lifeblood of the year —
What flamingo dawns have wavered from the east,
What eves have crimsoned to their toppling crest
To give the fame and transience that you wear!
Leaf-low he shall lie soon: but no such blaze
Briefly can cheer man's ashen, harsh decline;
His fall is short of pride, he bleeds within
And paler creeps to the dead end of his days.
O light's abandon and the fire-crest sky
Speak in me now for all who are to die!

February 1936

Infirm and grey
This leaden-hearted day
Drags its lank hours, wishing itself away.

Grey as the skin
Of long-imprisoned men
The sky, and holds a poisoned thought within.

Whether to die,
Or live beneath fear's eye —
Heavily hangs the sentence of this sky.

The unshed tears
Of frost on boughs and briers
Gathering wait discharge like our swoln fears.

Servant and host
Of this fog-bitter frost,
A carrion-crow flaps, shadowing the lost.

Now to the fire
From killing fells we bear
This new-born lamb, our premature desire.

We cannot meet
Our children's mirth, at night
Who dream their blood upon a darkening street.

Stay away, Spring!
Since death is on the wing
To blast our seed and poison every thing.

A Parting Shot

He said, 'Do not point your gun
At the dove in the judas tree:
It might go off, you see.'

So I fired, and the tree came down
Limed leaf, branch and stock,
And the fantail swerving flew
Up like a shuttlecock
Released into the blue.

And he said, 'I told you so'.

Newsreel

Enter the dream-house, brothers and sisters, leaving
Your debts asleep, your history at the door:
This is the home for heroes, and this loving
Darkness a fur you can afford.

Fish in their tank electrically heated
Nose without envy the glass wall: for them
Clerk, spy, nurse, killer, prince, the great and the defeated,
Move in a mute day-dream.

Bathed in this common source, you gape incurious
At what your active hours have willed —
Sleep-walking on that silver wall, the furious
Sick shapes and pregnant fancies of your world.

There is the mayor opening the oyster season:
A society wedding: the autumn hats look swell:
An old crocks' race, and a politician
In fishing-waders to prove that all is well.

Oh, look at the warplanes! Screaming hysteric treble
In the long power-dive, like gannets they fall steep.
But what are they to trouble —
These silver shadows to trouble your watery, womb-deep
        sleep?

See the big guns, rising, groping, erected
To plant death in your world's soft womb.
Fire-bud, smoke-blossom, iron seed projected —
Are these exotics? They will grow nearer home:

Grow nearer home — and out of the dream-house stumbling
One night into a strangling air and the flung
Rags of children and thunder of stone niagaras tumbling,
You'll know you slept too long.

From Regency Houses

We who in younger days,
Hoping too much, tried on
The habit of perfection,
Have learnt how it betrays
Our shrinking flesh: we have seen
The praised transparent will
Living now by reflection.
The panes darken: but still
We have seen peering out
The mad, too mobile face
Under the floral hat.
Are we living — we too,
Living extravagant farce
In the finery of spent passions?
Is all we do and shall do
But the glib, habitual breathing
Of clocks where time means nothing,
In a condemned mansion?

A Happy View

. . . So take a happy view —
This lawn graced with the candle-flames of crocus,
Frail-handed girls under the flowering chestnut,
Or anything will do
That time takes back before it seems untrue:

And, if the truth were told,
You'd count it luck, perceiving in what shallow
Crevices and few crumbling grains of comfort
Man's joy will seed, his cold
And hardy fingers find an eagle's hold.

Overtures to Death

1

For us, born into a world
Of fledged, instinctive trees,
Of lengthening days, snowfall at Christmas
And sentried palaces,

You were the one our parents
Could not forget or forgive —
A remittance man, a very very
Distant relative.

We read your name in the family
Bible. It was tabu
At meals and lessons, but in church sometimes
They seemed to be praying for you.

You lived overseas, we gathered:
And often lying safe
In bed we thought of you, hearing the indrawn
Breath of the outcast surf.

Later we heard them saying
You had done well in the War.
And, though you never came home to us,
We saw your name everywhere.

When home grew unsympathetic,
You were all the rage for a while —
The favourite uncle with the blank-cheque-book
And the understanding smile.

Some of us went to look for you
In aeroplanes and fast cars:
Some tried the hospitals, some took to vice,
Others consulted the stars.

But now, sir, that you may be going
To visit us any night,
We watch the french windows, picturing you
In rather a different light.

The house, we perceive, is shabby,
There's dry-rot in the wood:
It's a poor welcome and it won't keep you out
And we wish we had been good.

But there's no time now for spring-cleaning
Or mending the broken lock.
We are here in the shrouded drawing-room till
Your first, your final knock.

2

When all the sky is skimming
And lovers frisk in the hay,
When it's easy forgiving the dead or the living,
He is not so far away.

When love's hands are too hot, too cold,
And justice turns a deaf ear,
When springs congeal and the skies are sealed,
We know that he is near.

Now here was a property, on all sides
Considered quite imposing:
Take a good look round at house and grounds —
The mortgage is foreclosing.

Now Death he is the bailiff
And he sits in our best room
Appraising chintz and ornaments
And the child in the womb.

We were not shysters or loonies,
Our spirit was up to proof:
Simpler far is the reason for our
Notice to quit this roof.

We paid for our lease and rule of life
In hard cash; and one day
The news got through to you-know-who
That we'd ceased to pay our way.

Oh what will happen to our dear sons,
Our dreams of pensioned ease?
They are downed and shredded, for the wind we dreaded
Worries the blossom trees.

Oh Death he is the bailiff
And his men wait outside:
We shall sleep well in our handsome shell
While he auctions away our pride.

* * *

4

Forgive us, that we ever thought
You could with innocence be bought,
Or, puffed with queasy power, have tried
Your register to override.

Such diamond-faced and equal laws
Allow no chink or saving clause:
Besotted may-fly, bobbish wren
Count in your books as much as men.

No North-West Passage can be found
To sail those freezing capes around,
Nor no smooth by-pass ever laid
Shall that metropolis evade.

The tampering hand, the jealous eye
That overlooked our infancy —
Forgiven soon, they sank their trust
And our reproach into the dust.

We also, whom a bawdy spring
Tempted to order everything,
Shall shrink beneath your first caress
Into a modest nothingness.

The meshes of the imperious blood,
The wind-flown tower, the poet's word
Can catch no more than a weak sigh
And ghost of immortality.

O lord of leisure, since we know
Your image we shall ne'er outgrow,
Teach us the value of our stay
Lest we insult the living clay.

This clay that binds the roots of man
And firmly foots his flying span —
Only this clay can voice, invest,
Measure and frame our mortal best.

O lord of night, bid us beware
The wistful ghost that speaks us fair:
Once let him in — he clots the veins
And makes a still-birth of our pains.

Now we at last have crossed the line
Where earth's exuberant fields begin,
That green illusion in the sky
Born of our desert years can die.

No longer let predestined need
Cramp our design, or hunger breed
Its windy dreams, or life distil
Rare personal good from common ill.

Lord of us all, now it is true
That we are lords of all but you,
Teach us the order of our day
Lest we deface the honoured clay.

5

The sun came out in April,
The hawthorn in May:
We thought the year, like other years,
Would go the Christmas way.

In June we picked the clover,
And sea-shells in July:
There was no silence at the door,
No word from the sky.

A hand came out of August
And flicked his life away:
We had not time to bargain, mope,
Moralize, or pray.

Where he had been, was only
An effigy on a bed
To ask us searching questions or
Hear what we'd left unsaid.

Only that stained parchment
Set out what he had been —
A face we might have learned better,
But now must read unseen.

Thus he resigned his interest
And claims, all in a breath,
Leaving us the long office work
And winding-up of death:

The ordinary anguish,
The stairs, the awkward turn,
The bearers' hats like black mushrooms
Placed upon the lawn.

As a migrant remembers
The sting and warmth of home,
As the fruit bears out the blossom's word,
We remember him.

He loved the sun in April,
The hawthorn in May:
Our tree will not light up for him
Another Christmas Day.

* * *

7

For us, born into a still
Unsweetened world, of sparse
Breathing-room, alleys brackish as hell's pit
And heaven-accusing spires,

You were never far nor fable,
Judgement nor happy end:
We have come to think of you, mister, as
Almost the family friend.

Our kiddies play tag with you often
Among the tornado wheels;
Through fevered nights you sit up with them,
You serve their little meals.

You lean with us at street-corners,
We have met you in the mine;
Your eyes are the foundry's glare, you beckon
From the snake-tooth, sly machine.

Low in the flooded engine room,
High on the yawing steeple —
Wherever we are, we begin to fancy
That we're your chosen people.

They came to us with charity,
They came to us with whips,
They came with chains behind their back
And freedom on their lips:

Castle and field and city —
Ours is a noble land,
Let us work for its fame together, they said;
But we don't quite understand.

For they took the land and the credit,
Took virtue and double-crossed her;
They left us the scrag-end of the luck
And the brunt of their disaster.

And now like horses they fidget
Smelling death in the air:
But we are your chosen people, and
We've little to lose or fear.

When the time comes for a clearance,
When light brims over the hill,
Mister, you can rely on us
To execute your will.

In the Heart of Contemplatior

In the heart of contemplation —
Admiring, say, the frost-flowers of the white lilac,
Or lark's song busily sifting like sand-crystals
Through the pleased hourglass an afternoon of summer,

Or your beauty, dearer to me than these —
Discreetly a whisper in the ear,
The glance of one passing my window recall me
From lark, lilac, you, grown suddenly strangers.

In the plump and pastoral valley
Of a leisure time, among the trees like seabirds
Asleep on a glass calm, one shadow moves —
The sly reminder of the forgotten appointment.
All the shining pleasures, born to be innocent,
Grow dark with a truant's guilt:
The day's high heart falls flat, the oaks tremble,
And the shadow sliding over your face divides us.

In the act of decision only,
In the hearts cleared for action like lovers naked
For love, this shadow vanishes: there alone
There is nothing between our lives for it to thrive on.
You and I with lilac, lark and oak-leafed
Valley are bound together
As in the astounded clarity before death.
Nothing is innocent now but to act for life's sake.

Questions

How long will you keep this pose of self-confessed
And aspen hesitation
Dithering on the brink, obsessed
Immobilized by the feminine fascination
Of an image all your own,
Or doubting which is shadow, which is bone?

Will you wait womanish, while the flattering stream
Glosses your faults away?

Or would you find within that dream
Courage to break the dream, wisdom to say
That wisdom is not there?
Or is it simply the first shock you fear?

Do you need the horn in your ear, the hounds at your heel,
Gadflies to sting you sore,
The lightning's angry feint, and all
The horizon clouds boiling like lead, before
You'll risk your javelin dive
And pierce reflection's heart, and come alive?

Spring Song

Floods and the voluble winds
Have warned the dead away:
In swaying copse the willows
Wave their magic wands.

The sun is here to deal
With the dull decay we felt:
In field and square he orders
The vague shadows to heel.

The licence is renewed
And all roads lead to summer:
Good girls come to grief,
Fish to the springy rod.

Our thoughts like sailplanes go
To and fro sauntering
Along fantastic cloud-streets
On warmer currents' flow.

A larger appetite,
A tautening of the will,
The wild pony tamed,
The common gorse alight.

Now the bee finds the pollen,
The pale boy a cure:
Who cares if in the sequel
Cocky shall be crestfallen?

Behold the Swan

Behold the swan
Riding at her image, anchored there
Complacent, a water-lily upon
The ornamental water:
Queen of the mute October air,
She broods in that unbroken
Reverie of reed and water.

Now from the stricken
Pool she hoists and flurries,
And passes overhead
In hoarse, expressive flight:
Her wings bear hard
On the vibrant air: unhurried
The threat and pulse of wings, the throat
Levelled towards the horizon, see —
They are prophecy.

Song

It was not far through the pinewoods
That day to the lodge gate,
But far enough for the wind to phrase
My ten-year-long regret.

It was not far by the cornfield,
The tall ears looked alive:
But my heart, like corn, was broken for
A harvest I could not have.

From husk of words unspoken
I'll winnow a ripe seed:
From woods where love was shy to trespass
I'll learn the airs I need.

Oh here and unlamenting
Her graceful ghost shall shine —
In the heart mature as fruited fields,
The singing words of pine.

The Escapist

Before a rumour stirred, he fled the country
Preferring blank disgrace to any gesture
That could wipe out his failure with himself.
A warmer man no doubt had realized
His assets in our buoyant love, and taken
Some bonds to gild an unromantic exile.

Before their first reproach could reach his ears,
He had set up a private court, accepted
Full responsibility, and passed judgement.

The man whom later they reviled because
He would not face their music, was already
Self-flayed and branded in his heart for ever.

Before the story broke, he had sat down
To write it out, determined that no vestige
Of guilt be missed, no tiniest false inflection
Of heroism creep in to justify
The ugly tale. They said he was too proud to
Trust other hands even with his dishonour.

Before you heap quick-lime upon that felon
Memory, think how nothing you can do
Could touch his self-vindictiveness, and nothing
You did to cure the cowardice it avenged for.
Say, if you like, escape was in his blood —
Escape's as good a word as any other.

Passage from Childhood

His earliest memory, the mood
Fingered and frail as maidenhair,
Was this — a china cup somewhere
In a green, deep wood.
He lives to find again somewhere
That wood, that homely cup; to taste all
Its chill, imagined dews; to dare
The dangerous crystal.

Who can say what misfeatured elf
First led him into that lifelong
Passage of mirrors where, so young,
He saw himself.

Balanced as Blondin, more headstrong
Than baby Hercules, rare as a one-
Cent British Guiana, above the wrong
And common run?

He knew the secrecy of squirrels,
The foolish doves' antiphony,
And what wrens fear. He was gun-shy,
Hating all quarrels.
Life was a hostile land to spy,
Full of questions he dared not ask
Lest the answer in mockery
Or worse unmask.

Quick to injustice, quick he grew
This hermit and contorted shell.
Self-pity like a thin rain fell,
Fouling the view:
Then tree-trunks seemed wet roots of hell,
Wren or catkin might turn vicious,
The dandelion clock could tell
Nothing auspicious.

No exile has ever looked so glum
With the pines fretful overhead,
Yet he felt at home in the gothic glade —
More than at home.
You will forgive him that he played
Bumble-puppy on the small mossed lawn
All by himself for hours, afraid
Of being born.

Lying awake one night, he saw
Eternity stretched like a howl of pain:
He was tiny and terrible, a new pin
On a glacier's floor.
Very few they are who have lain
With eternity and lived to tell it:

There's a secret process in his brain
And he cannot sell it.

Now, beyond reach of sense or reason,
His life walks in a glacial sleep
For ever, since he drank that cup
And found it poison.
He's one more ghost, engaged to keep
Eternity's long hours and mewed
Up in live flesh with no escape
From solitude.

Self-Criticism and Answer

It was always so, always —
My too meticulous words
Mocked by the unhinged cries
Of playground, mouse or gull,
By throats of nestling birds
Like bells upturned in a peal —
All that has innocence
To praise and far to fall.

I fear this careful art
Would never storm the sense:
Its agonies are but the eager
Retching of an empty heart;
It never was possessed
By divine incontinence,
And for him whom that eygre
Sweeps not, silence were best.

Your politicians pray silence
For the ribald trumpeter,

The falsetto crook, the twitching
Unappeasable dictator.
For any else you should be pleased
To hold your tongue: but Satan
Himself would disown his teaching
And turn to spit on these.

When madmen play the piper
And knaves call the tune,
Honesty's a right passion —
She must call to her own.
Let yours be the start and stir
Of a flooding indignation
That channels the dry heart deeper
And sings through the dry bone.

From Word Over All (1943)

To Rosamond Lehmann

Word over all, beautiful as the sky,
Beautiful that war and all its deeds of carnage must
*   in time be utterly lost,*
That the hands of the sisters Death and Night
*   incessantly softly wash again, and ever again, this*
*   soiled world.*

WALT WHITMAN

The Lighted House

One night they saw the big house, some time untenanted
But for its hand-to-mouth recluse, room after room
Light up, as when Primavera herself has spirited
A procession of crocuses out of their winter tomb.

Revels unearthly are going forward, one did remark—
He has conjured a thing of air or fire for his crazed delight:
Another said, It is only a traveller lost in the dark
He welcomes for mercy's sake. Each, in a way, was right.

You were the magic answer, the sprite fire-fingered who came
To lighten my heart, my house, my heirlooms; you are the wax
That melts at my touch and still supports my prodigal flame:

But you were also the dead-beat traveller out of the storm
Returned to yourself by almost obliterated tracks,
Peeling off fear after fear, revealing love's true form.

The Album

I see you, a child
In a garden sheltered for buds and playtime,
Listening as if beguiled
By a fancy beyond your years and the flowering maytime.
The print is faded: soon there will be
No trace of that pose enthralling,
Nor visible echo of my voice distantly calling
'Wait! Wait for me!'

Then I turn the page
To a girl who stands like a questioning iris

By the waterside, at an age
That asks every mirror to tell what the heart's desire is.
The answer she finds in that oracle stream
Only time could affirm or disprove,
Yet I wish I was there to venture a warning, 'Love
Is not what you dream.'

Next you appear
As if garlands of wild felicity crowned you —
Courted, caressed, you wear
Like immortelles the lovers and friends around you.
'They will not last you, rain or shine,
They are but straws and shadows,'
I cry: 'Give not to those charming desperadoes
What was made to be mine.'

One picture is missing —
The last. It would show me a tree stripped bare
By intemperate gales, her amazing
Noonday of blossom spoilt which promised so fair.
Yet, scanning those scenes at your heyday taken,
I tremble, as one who must view
In the crystal a doom he could never deflect — yes, I too
Am fruitlessly shaken.

I close the book;
But the past slides out of its leaves to haunt me
And it seems, wherever I look,
Phantoms of irreclaimable happiness taunt me.
Then I see her, petalled in new-blown hours,
Beside me — 'All you love most there
Has blossomed again,' she murmurs, 'all that you missed there
Has grown to be yours.'

The Hunter's Game

I am an arrow, I am a bow —
The bow sings fierce and deep,
The arrow's tipped with cruel flame,
Feathered with passionate sleep.
When you play the hunter's game,
I am your arrow and your bow.

Only my love can bend the bow:
When the bow leaps to kill
And darkly as a nerve of night
The string throbs out, you are the skill
That drew the impulsive bowstring tight,
The hand that bent the bow.

What is the air that floats my arrow
Smoothly aloft and bears
It up to the sun, down to the dark?
You are the wanton airs
Which shape and hold its shining arc,
The innocent air that flights the arrow.

What is the victim of this arrow
That flies so fast and true?
Deep in the close, fawn-dappled glade,
Pierced by a shaft of light are you
The huntress, white and smiling, laid —
The victim of your arrow.

Departure in the Dark

Nothing so sharply reminds a man he is mortal
As leaving a place
In a winter morning's dark, the air on his face
Unkind as the touch of sweating metal:
Simple goodbyes to children or friends become
A felon's numb
Farewell, and love that was a warm, a meeting place —
Love is the suicide's grave under the nettles.

Gloomed and clemmed as if by an imminent ice-age
Lies the dear world
Of your street-strolling, field-faring. The senses, curled
At the dead end of a shrinking passage,
Care not if close the inveterate hunters creep,
And memories sleep
Like mammoths in lost caves. Drear, extinct is the world,
And has no voice for consolation or presage.

There is always something at such times of the passover,
When the dazed heart
Beats for it knows not what, whether you part
From home or prison, acquaintance or lover —
Something wrong with the time-table, something unreal
In the scrambled meal
And the bag ready packed by the door, as though the heart
Has gone ahead, or is staying here for ever.

No doubt for the Israelites that early morning
It was hard to be sure
If home were prison or prison home: the desire
Going forth meets the desire returning.
This land, that had cut their pride down to the bone
Was now their own
By ancient deeds of sorrow. Beyond, there was nothing sure
But a desert of freedom to quench their fugitive yearnings.

At this blind hour the heart is informed of nature's
Ruling that man
Should be nowhere a more tenacious settler than
Among wry thorns and ruins, yet nurture
A seed of discontent in his ripest ease.
There's a kind of release
And a kind of torment in every goodbye for every man
And will be, even to the last of his dark departures.

Cornet Solo

Thirty years ago lying awake,   /
Lying awake
In London at night when childhood barred me
From livelier pastimes, I'd hear a street-band break
Into old favourites — 'The Ash Grove', 'Killarney'
Or 'Angels Guard Thee'.

That was the music for such an hour —
A deciduous hour
Of leaf-wan drizzle, of solitude
And gaslight bronzing the gloom like an autumn flower —
The time and music for a boy imbrued
With the pensive mood.

I could have lain for hours together,
Sweet hours together,
Listening to the cornet's cry
Down wet streets gleaming like patent leather
Where beauties jaunted in cabs to their revelry,
Jewelled and spry.

Plaintive its melody rose or waned
Like an autumn wind
Blowing the rain on beds of aster,

On man's last bed: mournful and proud it complained
As a woman who dreams of the charms that graced her,
In young days graced her.

Strange how those yearning airs could sweeten
And still enlighten
The hours when solitude gave me her breast.
Strange they could tell a mere child how hearts may beat in
The self-same tune for the once-possessed
And the unpossessed.

Last night, when I heard a cornet's strain,
It seemed a refrain
Wafted from thirty years back — so remote an
Echo it bore: but I felt again
The prophetic mood of a child, too long forgotten,
Too lightly forgotten.

O Dreams, O Destinations

1

For infants time is like a humming shell
Heard between sleep and sleep, wherein the shores
Foam-fringed, wind-fluted of the strange earth dwell
And the sea's cavernous hunger faintly roars.
It is the humming pole of summer lanes
Whose sound quivers like heat-haze endlessly
Over the corn, over the poppied plains —
An emanation from the earth or sky.
Faintly they hear, through the womb's lingering haze,
A rumour of that sea to which they are born:
They hear the ringing pole of summer days,

But need not know what hungers for the corn.
They are the lisping rushes in a stream —
Grace-notes of a profound, legato dream.

2

Children look down upon the morning-grey
Tissue of mist that veils a valley's lap:
Their fingers itch to tear it and unwrap
The flags, the roundabouts, the gala day.
They watch the spring rise inexhaustibly —
A breathing thread out of the eddied sand,
Sufficient to their day: but half their mind
Is on the sailed and glittering estuary.
Fondly we wish their mist might never break,
Knowing it hides so much that best were hidden:
We'd chain them by the spring, lest it should broaden
For them into a quicksand and a wreck.
But they slip through our fingers like the source,
Like mist, like time that has flagged out their course.

3

That was the fatal move, the ruination
Of innocence so innocently begun,
When in the lawless orchard of creation
The child left this fruit for that rosier one.
Reaching towards the far thing, we begin it;
Looking beyond, or backward, more and more
We grow unfaithful to the unique minute
Till, from neglect, its features stale and blur.
Fish, bird or beast was never thus unfaithful —
Man only casts the image of his joys
Beyond his senses' reach; and by this fateful
Act, he confirms the ambiguous power of choice.
Innocence made that first choice. It is she
Who weeps, a child chained to the outraged tree.

4

Our youthtime passes down a colonnade
Shafted with alternating light and shade.
All's dark or dazzle there. Half in a dream
Rapturously we move, yet half afraid
Never to wake. That diamond-point, extreme
Brilliance engraved on us a classic theme:
The shaft of darkness had its lustre too,
Rising where earth's concentric mysteries gleam.
Oh youth-charmed hours, that made an avenue
Of fountains playing us on to love's full view,
A cypress walk to some romantic grave —
Waking, how false in outline and in hue
We find the dreams that flickered on our cave:
Only your fire, which cast them, still seems true.

5

All that time there was thunder in the air:
Our nerves branched and flickered with summer lightning.
The taut crab-apple, the pampas quivering, the glare
On the roses seemed irrelevant, or a heightening
At most of the sealed-up hour wherein we awaited
What? — some explosive oracle to abash
The platitudes on the lawn? heaven's delegated
Angel — the golden rod, our burning bush?
No storm broke. Yet in retrospect the rose
Mounting vermilion, fading, glowing again
Like a fire's heart, that breathless inspiration
Of pampas grass, crab-tree's attentive pose
Never were so divinely charged as then —
The veiled Word's flesh, a near annunciation.

6

Symbols of gross experience! — our grief
Flowed, like a sacred river, underground:

Desire bred fierce abstractions on the mind,
Then like an eagle soared beyond belief.
Often we tried our breast against the thorn,
Our paces on the turf: whither we flew,
Why we should agonize, we hardly knew —
Nor what ached in us, asking to be born.
Ennui of youth! — thin air above the clouds,
Vain divination of the sunless stream
Mirror that impotence, till we redeem
Our birthright, and the shadowplay concludes.
Ah, not in dreams, but when our souls engage
With the common mesh and moil, we come of age.

7

Older, we build a road where once our active
Heat threw up mountains and the deep dales veined:
We're glad to gain the limited objective,
Knowing the war we fight in has no end.
The road must needs follow each contour moulded
By that fire in its losing fight with earth:
We march over our past, we may behold it
Dreaming a slave's dream on our bivouac hearth.
Lost the archaic dawn wherein we started,
The appetite for wholeness: now we prize
Half-loaves, half-truths — enough for the half-hearted,
The gleam snatched from corruption satisfies.
Dead youth, forgive us if, all but defeated,
We raise a trophy where your honour lies.

8

But look, the old illusion still returns,
Walking a field-path where the succory burns
Like summer's eye, blue lustre-drops of noon,
And the heart follows it and freshly yearns:
Yearns to the sighing distances beyond
Each height of happiness, the vista drowned

In gold-dust haze, and dreams itself immune
From change and night to which all else is bound.
Love, we have caught perfection for a day
As succory holds a gem of halcyon ray:
Summer burns out, its flower will tarnish soon —
Deathless illusion, that could so relay
The truth of flesh and spirit, sun and clay
Singing for once together all in tune!

9

To travel like a bird, lightly to view
Deserts where stone gods founder in the sand,
Ocean embraced in a white sleep with land;
To escape time, always to start anew.
To settle like a bird, make one devoted
Gesture of permanence upon the spray
Of shaken stars and autumns; in a bay
Beyond the crestfallen surges to have floated.
Each is our wish. Alas, the bird flies blind,
Hooded by a dark sense of destination:
Her weight on the glass calm leaves no impression,
Her home is soon a basketful of wind.
Travellers, we're fabric of the road we go;
We settle, but like feathers on time's flow.

Word Over All

Now when drowning imagination clutches
At old loves drifting away,
Splintered highlights, hope capsized — a wrecked world's
Flotsam, what can I say
To cheer the abysmal gulfs, the crests that lift not
To any land in sight?
How shall the sea-waif, who lives from surge to surge, chart
Current and reef aright?

Always our time's ghost-guise of impermanence
Daunts me: whoever I meet,
Wherever I stand, a shade of parting lengthens
And laps around my feet.
But now, the heart-sunderings, the real migrations —
Millions fated to flock
Down weeping roads to mere oblivion — strike me
Dumb as a rooted rock.

I watch when searchlights set the low cloud smoking
Like acid on metal: I start
At sirens, sweat to feel a whole town wince
And thump, a terrified heart,
Under the bomb-strokes. These, to look back on, are
A few hours' unrepose:
But the roofless old, the child beneath the debris —
How can I speak for those?

Busy the preachers, the politicians weaving
Voluble charms around
This ordeal, conjuring a harvest that shall spring from
Our hearts' all-harrowed ground.
I, who chose to be caged with the devouring
Present, must hold its eye
Where blaze ten thousand farms and fields unharvested,
And hearts, steel-broken, die.

Yet words there must be, wept on the cratered present,
To gleam beyond it:
Never was cup so mortal but poets with mild
Everlastings have crowned it.
See wavelets and wind-blown shadows of leaves on a stream
How they ripple together,
As life and death intermarried — you cannot tell
One from another.

Our words like poppies love the maturing field,
But form no harvest:

May lighten the innocent's pang, or paint the dreams
Where guilt is unharnessed.
Dark over all, absolving all, is hung
Death's vaulted patience:
Words are to set man's joy and suffering there
In constellations.

We speak of what we know, but what we have spoken
Truly we know not —
Whether our good may tarnish, our grief to far
Centuries glow not.
The Cause shales off, the Humankind stands forth
A mightier presence,
Flooded by dawn's pale courage, rapt in eve's
Rich acquiescence.

The Poet

For me there is no dismay
Though ills enough impend.
I have learned to count each day
Minute by breathing minute —
Birds that lightly begin it,
Shadows muting its end —
As lovers count for luck
Their own heart-beats and believe
In the forest of time they pluck
Eternity's single leaf.

Tonight the moon's at the full.
Full moon's the time for murder.
But I look to the clouds that hide her —
The bay below me is dull,
An unreflecting glass —

And chafe for the clouds to pass,
And wish she suddenly might
Blaze down at me so I shiver
Into a twelve-branched river
Of visionary light.

For now imagination,
My royal, impulsive swan,
With raking flight — I can see her —
Comes down as it were upon
A lake in whirled snow-floss
And flurry of spray like a skier
Checking. Again I feel
The wounded waters heal.
Never before did she cross
My heart with such exaltation.

Oh, on this striding edge,
This hare-bell height of calm
Where intuitions swarm
Like nesting gulls and knowledge
Is free as the winds that blow,
A little while sustain me,
Love, till my answer is heard!
Oblivion roars below,
Death's cordon narrows: but vainly,
If I've slipped the carrier word.

Dying, any man may
Feel wisdom harmonious, fateful
At the tip of his dry tongue.
All I have felt or sung
Seems now but the moon's fitful
Sleep on a clouded bay,
Swan's maiden flight, or the climb
To a tremulous, hare-bell crest.
Love, tear the song from my breast!
Short, short is the time.

Watching Post

A hill flank overlooking the Axe valley.
Among the stubble a farmer and I keep watch
For whatever may come to injure our countryside —
Light-signals, parachutes, bombs, or sea-invaders.
The moon looks over the hill's shoulder, and hope
Mans the old ramparts of an English night.

In a house down there was Marlborough born. One night
Monmouth marched to his ruin out of that valley.
Beneath our castled hill, where Britons kept watch,
Is a church where the Drakes, old lords of this countryside,
Sleep under their painted effigies. No invaders
Can dispute their legacy of toughness and hope.

Two counties away, over Bristol, the searchlights hope
To find what danger is in the air tonight.
Presently gunfire from Portland reaches our valley
Tapping like an ill-hung door in a draught. My watch
Says nearly twelve. All over the countryside
Moon-dazzled men are peering out for invaders.

The farmer and I talk for a while of invaders:
But soon we turn to crops — the annual hope,
Making of cider, prizes for ewes. Tonight
How many hearts along this war-mazed valley
Dream of a day when at peace they may work and watch
The small sufficient wonders of the countryside.

Image or fact, we both in the countryside
Have found our natural law, and until invaders
Come will answer its need: for both of us, hope
Means a harvest from small beginnings, who this night
While the moon sorts out into shadow and shape our valley,
A farmer and a poet, are keeping watch.

July, 1940

Where are the War Poets?

They who in folly or mere greed
Enslaved religion, markets, laws,
Borrow our language now and bid
Us to speak up in freedom's cause.

It is the logic of our times,
No subject for immortal verse —
That we who lived by honest dreams
Defend the bad against the worse.

Angel

We thought the angel of death would come
As a thundering judge to impeach us,
So we practised an attitude of calm or indignation
And prepared the most eloquent speeches.

But when the angel of death stepped down,
She was like a spoilt girl in ermine:
She tipped a negligent wing to some
And treated the rest as vermin.

Now we have seen the way she goes on,
Our self-possession wavers:
We'd fear a hanging judge far less than
That bitch's casual favours.

Lidice

Not a grave of the murdered for freedom but grows seed for freedom.
WALT WHITMAN

Cry to us, murdered village. While your grave
Aches raw on history, make us understand
What freedom asks of us. Strengthen our hand
Against the arrogant dogmas that deprave
And have no proof but death at their command.

Must the innocent bleed for ever to remedy
These fanatic fits that tear mankind apart?
The pangs we felt from your atrocious hurt
Promise a time when even the killer shall see
His sword is aimed at his own naked heart.

Ode to Fear

The lustre bowl of the sky
Sounds and sustains
A throbbing cello-drone of planes.
Entombed beneath this caving liberty,
We note how doom endorses
Our devious fraud and folly where skeins
Of wild geese flew direct on visionary courses.

Now Fear has come again
To live with us
In poisoned intimacy like pus,
Hourly extending the area of our pain,
It seems I must make the most
Of fever's pulsing dreams and thus
Live to allay this evil or dying lay its ghost.

Fear has so many symptoms —
Planes throbbing above
Like headache, rumours that glibly move
Along the bloodstream, sleep's prophetic phantoms
Condemning what we have built,
Heartburn anxiety for those we love —
And all, yes all, are proof of an endemic guilt.

The bones, the stalwart spine,
The legs like bastions,
The nerves, the heart's natural combustions,
The head that hives our active thoughts — all pine,
Are quenched or paralysed
When Fear puts unexpected questions
And makes the heroic body freeze like a beast surprised.

The sap will rise anew in
Both man and brute:
Wild virtues even now can shoot
From the reviled interstices of ruin.
But oh, what drug, what knife
Can wither up our guilt at the root,
Cure our discoloured days and cleanse the blood of life?

Today, I can but record
In truth and patience
This high delirium of nations
And hold to it the reflecting, fragile word.
Come to my heart then, Fear,
With all your linked humiliations,
As wild geese flight and settle on a submissive mere.

Reconciliation

All day beside the shattered tank he'd lain
Like a limp creature hacked out of its shell,
Now shrivelling on the desert's grid,
Now floating above a sharp-set ridge of pain.

There came a roar, like water, in his ear.
The mortal dust was laid. He seemed to be lying
In a cool coffin of stone walls,
While memory slid towards a plunging weir.

The time that was, the time that might have been
Find in this shell of stone a chance to kiss
Before they part eternally:
He feels a world without, a world within

Wrestle like old antagonists, until each is
Balancing each. Then, in a heavenly calm,
The lock gates open, and beyond
Appear the argent, swan-assemblied reaches.

The Innocent

A forward child, a sullen boy,
My living image in the pool,
The glass that made me look a fool —
He was my judgement and my joy.

The bells that chimed above the lake,
The swans asleep in evening's eye,
Bright transfers pressed on memory
From him their gloss and anguish take.

When I was desolate, he came
A wizard way to charm my toys:
But when he heard a stranger's voice
He broke the toys, I bore the shame.

I built a house of crystal tears
Amid the myrtles for my friend:
He said, no man has ever feigned
Or kept the lustre of my years.

Later, a girl and I descried
His shadow on the fern-flecked hill,
His double near our bed: and still
The more I lived, the more he died.

Now a revenant slips between
The fine-meshed minutes of the clock
To weep the time we lost and mock
All that my desperate ditties mean.

Hornpipe

Now the peak of summer's past, the sky is overcast
And the love we swore would last for an age seems deceit:
Paler is the guelder since the day we first beheld her
In blush beside the elder drifting sweet, drifting sweet.

Oh quickly they fade — the sunny esplanade,
Speed-boats, wooden spades, and the dunes where we've lain:
Others will be lying amid the sea-pinks sighing
For love to be undying, and they'll sigh in vain.

It's hurrah for each night we have spent our love so lightly
And never dreamed there might be no more to spend at all.

It's goodbye to every lover who thinks he'll live in clover
All his life, for noon is over soon and night-dews fall.

If I could keep you there with the berries in your hair
And your lacy fingers fair as the may, sweet may,
I'd have no heart to do it, for to stay love is to rue it
And the harder we pursue it, the faster it's away.

The Fault

After the light decision
Made by the blood in a moon-blanched lane,
Whatever weariness or contrition
May come, I could never see you plain;
No, never again

See you whose body I'm wed to
Distinct, but always dappled, enhanced
By a montage of all that moment led to —
Dunes where heat-haze and sea-pinks glanced,
The roads that danced

Ahead of our aimless car,
Scandal biting the dust behind us,
The feel of being on a luckier star,
Each quarrel that came like a night to blind us
And closer to bind us.

Others will journey over
Our hill up along this lane like a rift
Loaded with moon-gold, many a lover
Sleepwalking through the moon's white drift,
Loved or bereft.

But for me it is love's volcanic
Too fertile fault, and will mark always
The first shock of that yielding mood, where satanic
Bryony twines and frail flowers blaze
Through our tangled days.

The Rebuke

Down in the lost and April days
What lies we told, what lies we told!
Nakedness seemed the one disgrace,
And there'd be time enough to praise
The truth when we were old.

The irresponsible poets sung
What came into their head:
Time to pick and choose among
The bold profusions of our tongue
When we were dead, when we were dead.

Oh wild the words we uttered then
In woman's ear, in woman's ear,
Believing all we promised when
Each kiss created earth again
And every far was near.

Little we guessed, who spoke the word
Of hope and freedom high
Spontaneously as wind or bird
To crowds like cornfields still or stirred,
It was a lie, a heart-felt lie.

Now the years advance into
A calmer stream, a colder stream,

We doubt the flame that once we knew,
Heroic words sound all untrue
As love-lies in a dream.

Yet fools are the old who won't be taught
Modesty by their youth:
That pandemonium of the heart,
That sensual arrogance did impart
A kind of truth, a kindling truth.

Where are the sparks at random sown,
The spendthrift fire, the holy fire?
Who cares a damn for truth that's grown
Exhausted haggling for its own
And speaks without desire?

From Poems 1943-1947 (1948)

To Laurie Lee

I seem but a dead man held on end
To sink down soon . . .
THOMAS HARDY

Le vent se lève . . . il faut tenter de vivre!
PAUL VALÉRY

Juvenilia

So this is you
That was an I twenty-five years ago —
One I may neither disown nor renew.
Youth of the smouldering heart, the seamless brow,
What affinity between you and me?
You are a skin I have long since cast,
A ghost I carry now:
I am the form you blindly, fitfully glassed,
And the finish of your bright vow.

When I seek to peer
Through the fancy-dress words wherein you are woodenly
        posed
And to feel the ardours quivering there,
I am as one eavesdropping upon a captive past
Of which nothing remains but echoes and chains.
Yet, could I lay bare that primitive mural
Whereon I am superimposed,
What boldness of line and colour, what pure quaint moral
Emblems might be disclosed!

Youth of the seamless brow, the smouldering heart,
You are my twin,
Yet we seem worlds apart.
More than mere time-grains pile this desert between:
The sands that efface each instant trace
Of my passage — I think they proceed
From my own nature, their origin
Some inexhaustible need
For oblivion, and reservoir of it, deep within.

Were it not so, surely I could remember
The lyric light,
The primrose-and-violet ember

Which was your soul, my soul, when we came to write
These poems. But gone is the breath of dawn,
Clinker the dreams it fanned:
These bones, anonymous now and trite,
Are a message scrawled on the sand
That only in dying could a self indite.

What links the real to the wraith?
My self repudiates myself of yesterday;
But the words it lived in and cast like a shell keep faith
With that dead self always.
And if aught holds true between me and you,
It is the heart whose prism can break
Life's primal rays
Into a spectrum of passionate tones, and awake
Fresh blossom for truth to swell and sway.

Speak to me, then, from the haunted
Hollow of fears and yearnings lost to view,
The instrument my youth, your truth, first sounded —
This heart of impassioned hue!
Speak through the crystal, tell me the gist
Of the shadowy sequence that now is I —
What unseen clue
Threads my pearl-sliding hours, what symmetry
My deaths and metaphors pursue!

When a phoenix opens her rainbow span,
The ashes she rose from warmly speak,
'Your flight, which ends in fire as it began,
Is fuelled by all you seek.'
O beacon bird, I too am fired
To bring some message home
Whose meaning I know not. So from peak to peak
I run — my life, maybe, a palindrome,
But each lap unique.

And since at every stage I need
A death, a new self to reveal me,

And only through oblivion's veil can read
The signs of what befell me,
May not the grave of rigored love
Be but one more abyss
Between two peaks, appointed to compel me
Along the chain of light? . . . Dead youth, is this
What you have to tell me?

Marriage of Two

So they were married, and lived
Happily for ever?
Such extravagant claims are not in heaven's gift —
Much less earth's, where love is chanceful as weather:
Say they were married, and lived.

Tell me his marriage vow.
Not the church responses,
But alone at a window one night saying, 'Now
Let me be good to her, all my heart owns or wants is
Staked on this hazardous vow.'

When was the marriage sealed?
One day the strange creature
He loved was missing; he found her, concealed
In a coign of, wearing the secret stamp of his nature.
So matings, if ever, are sealed.

How did the marriage end?
Some marriages die not.
The government goes into exile; then
The underground struggle is on, whose fighters fly not
Even at the bitter end.

What is the marriage of two?
The loss of one
By wounds or abdication; a true
Surrender mocked, an unwished victory won:
Rose, desert — mirage too.

The Woman Alone

1

Take any place — this garden plot will do
Where he with mower, scythe or hook goes out
To fight the grass and lay a growing fever,
Volcanic for another, dead to me;
Meek is the ghost, a banked furnace the man.

Take any time — this autumn day will serve,
Ripe with grassed fruit, raw with departing wings,
When I, whom in my youth the season tempted
To oceanic amplitudes, bend down
And pick a rotting apple from the grass.

From every here and now a thread leads back
Through faithless seasons and devouring seas:
New blooms, dead leaves bury it not, nor combers
Break it — my life line and my clue: the same
That brought him safe out of a labyrinth.

So I, the consort of an absent mind,
The emerald lost in a green waste of time,
The castaway for whom all space is island —
To follow, find, escape, this thread in hand,
Warp myself out upon the swelling past.

2

Take any joy — the thread leads always on
To here and now: snow, silence, vertigo;
His frozen face, a woman who bewails not
Only because she fears one echoing word
May bring the avalanche about her ears.

Take any joy that was — here it remains,
Corruptless, irrecoverable, cold
As a dead smile, beneath the cruel glacier
That moved upon our kisses, lambs and leaves,
Stilled them, but will not let their forms dissolve.

O tomb transparent of my waxen joys!
O lifelike dead under the skin of ice!
O frozen face of love where my one treasure
Is locked, and the key lost! May I not share
Even the bare oblivion of your fate?

But dare I throw the past into one fire,
One burning cry to break the silence, break
The cataleptic snows, the dream of falling?
Last night I thought he stood beside my bed
And said, 'Wake up! You were dreaming. I am here.'

3

Take any grief — the maggot at the nerve,
The words that bore the skull like waterdrops,
The castaway's upon the foam-racked island,
The lurching figures of a mind's eclipse —
I have felt each and all as love decayed.

Yet every grief revives a fainting love.
They are love's children too; I live again
In them; my breast yearns to their innocent cruelty.
If only tears can float a stranded heart,
If only sighs can move it, I will grieve.

The pleasured nerve, the small-talk in the night,
The voyaging when isles were daisy-chains,
The dance of mere routine — if I could reach them
Again through this sick labyrinth of grief,
I would rejoice in it, to reach them so.

Alas, hull-down upon hope's ashen verge
Hastens the vessel that our joined hands launched,
Stretching my heart-strings out beyond endurance.
Ah, will they never snap? Can I not climb
The signal hill, and wave, and *mean* goodbye?

Ending

That it should end so! —
Not with mingling tears
Nor one long backward look of woe
Towards a sinking trust,
A heyday's afterglow;
Not even in the lash and lightning
Cautery of rage!
But by this slow
Fissure, this blind numb grinding severance
Of floe from floe.
Merciless god, to mock your failures so!

Statuette: Late Minoan

Girl of the musing mouth,
The mild archaic air,
For whom do you subtly smile?
Yield to what power or prayer
Breasts vernally bare?

I seem to be peering at you
Through the wrong end of time
That shrinks to a bright, far image —
Great Mother of earth's prime —
A stature sublime.

So many golden ages
Of sunshine steeped your clay,
So dear did the maker cherish
In you life's fostering ray,
That you warm us today.

Goddess or girl, you are earth.
The smile, the offered breast —
They were the dream of one
Thirsting as I for rest,
As I, unblest.

The Heartsease

Do you remember that hour
In a nook of the flowing uplands
When you found for me, at the cornfield's edge,
A golden and purple flower?
Heartsease, you said. I thought it might be
A token that love meant well by you and me.

I shall not find it again
With you no more to guide me.
I could not bear to find it now
With anyone else beside me.
And the heartsease is far less rare
Than what it is named for, what I can feel nowhere.

Once again it is summer:
Wildflowers beflag the lane
That takes me away from our golden uplands,
Heart-wrung and alone.
The best I can look for, by vale or hill,
A herb they tell me is common enough — self-heal.

Emily Brontë

All is the same still. Earth and heaven locked in
A wrestling dream the seasons cannot break:
Shrill the wind tormenting my obdurate thorn trees,
Moss-rose and stone-chat silent in its wake.
Time has not altered here the rhythms I was rocked in,
Creation's throb and ache.

All is yet the same, for mine was a country
Stoic, unregenerate, beyond the power
Of man to mollify or God to disburden —
An ingrown landscape none might long endure
But one who could meet with a passion wilder-wintry
The scalding breath of the moor.

All is yet the same as when I roved the heather
Chained to a demon through the shrieking night,
Took him by the throat while he flailed my sibylline
Assenting breast, and won him to delight.
O truth and pain immortally bound together!
O lamp the storm made bright!

Still on those heights prophetic winds are raving,
Heath and harebell intone a plainsong grief:
'Shrink, soul of man, shrink into your valleys —
Too sharp that agony, that spring too brief!
Love, though your love is but the forged engraving
Of hope on a stricken leaf!'

Is there one whom blizzards warm and rains enkindle
And the bitterest furnace could no more refine?
Anywhere one too proud for consolation,
Burning for pure freedom so that he will pine,
Yes, to the grave without her? Let him mingle
His barren dust with mine.

But is there one who faithfully has planted
His seed of light in the heart's deepest scar?
When the night is darkest, when the wind is keenest,
He, he shall find upclimbing from afar
Over his pain my chaste, my disenchanted
And death-rebuking star.

Who Goes There?

(For Walter de la Mare, on his 75th birthday)

Who goes there?
What sequestered vale at the back of beyond
Do you come from — you with the moonbeam wand,
The innocent air?
And how got you here, spirited on like a bubble of silence
    past
The quickset ears, the hair-trigger nerves at each post?

    My staff is cut from the knowledge tree.
    My place no infidel eye can see.
    My way is a nonchalant one,
    Wilful as wind yet true as the line of a bee.
    My name is —Anon.

Are you aware
That you're trespassing, sir, on a battleground?
It's hard to see what excuse can be found
For magicians where
All light and airy ways must endanger the men's morale.
What business have you with the sturdy ranks of the real?

    I bring them dew from earth's dayspring.
    Fire from the first wild rose I bring.

And this — my deepest art —
I bring them word from their own hungering
Beleaguered heart.

Pass, friend. You bear
Gifts that, although men commonly flout them
Being hardened, or born, to live without them,
Are none the less rare.
Pass, friend, and fare you well, and may all such travellers
    be speeded
Who bring us news we had almost forgot we needed.

Lines for Edmund Blunden on his Fiftieth Birthday

Your fiftieth birthday. What shall we give you?
    An illuminated address
Would be hard on one who was never at home with
    Pomp or pretentiousness.
Here is a loving-cup made from verse,
    For verse is your favourite of metals:
Imagine its stem like a tulip stalk,
    Its bowl a tulip's petals
And the whole as gracefully formed and charactered
    As a poem of your own.
What shall the toast be? Fifty years more?
    A century? Let it be known
That a true poet's age is truthfully reckoned
    Not in years but in song:
So we drink instead to that happy girl
    Your Muse — may she live long!
But we pledge our love, our love for one
    Who never has burned or bowed

To popular gods, and when fame beckons
   Modestly melts in the crowd.
Into the crowd of your haunting fancies —
   The streams, the airs, the dews,
The soldier shades and the solacing heartbeams —
   You melt, and fame pursues;
And our good wishes follow you, even
   To the fortunate meadows where
Tonight your loving-cup is raised
   By Shelley, Hunt and Clare.

A Hard Frost

A frost came in the night and stole my world
And left this changeling for it — a precocious
Image of spring, too brilliant to be true:
White lilac on the windowpane, each grass-blade
Furred like a catkin, maydrift loading the hedge.
The elms behind the house are elms no longer
But blossomers in crystal, stems of the mist
That hangs yet in the valley below, amorphous
As the blind tissue whence creation formed.
   The sun looks out, and the fields blaze with diamonds.
Mockery spring, to lend this bridal gear
For a few hours to a raw country maid,
Then leave her all disconsolate with old fairings
Of aconite and snowdrop! No, not here
Amid this flounce and filigree of death
Is the real transformation scene in progress,
But deep below where frost
Worrying the stiff clods unclenches their
Grip on the seed and lets our future breathe.

The Christmas Tree

Put out the lights now!
Look at the Tree, the rough tree dazzled
In oriole plumes of flame,
Tinselled with twinkling frost fire, tasselled
With stars and moons — the same
That yesterday hid in the spinney and had no fame
Till we put out the lights now.

Hard are the nights now:
The fields at moonrise turn to agate,
Shadows are cold as jet;
In dyke and furrow, in copse and faggot
The frost's tooth is set;
And stars are the sparks whirled out by the north wind's fret
On the flinty nights now.

So feast your eyes now
On mimic star and moon-cold bauble:
Worlds may wither unseen,
But the Christmas Tree is a tree of fable,
A phoenix in evergreen,
And the world cannot change or chill what its mysteries
     mean
To your hearts and eyes now.

The vision dies now
Candle by candle: the tree that embraced it
Returns to its own kind,
To be earthed again and weather as best it
May the frost and the wind.
Children, it too had its hour — you will not mind
If it lives or dies now.

The Chrysanthemum Show

Here's Abbey Way: here are the rooms
   Where they held the chrysanthemum show —
Leaves like talons of greenfire, blooms
Of a barbarous frenzy, red, flame, bronze —
And a schoolboy walked in the furnace once,
   Thirty years ago.

You might have thought, had you seen him that day
   Mooching from stall to stall,
It was wasted on him — the prize array
Of flowers with their resinous, caustic tang,
Their colours that royally boomed and rang
   Like gongs in the pitchpine hall.

Any tongue could scorch him; even hope tease
   As if it dissembled a leer:
Like smouldering fuse, anxieties
Blindwormed his breast. How should one feel,
Consuming in youth's slow ordeal,
   What flashes from flower to flower?

Yet something did touch him then, at the quick,
   Like a premature memory prising
Through flesh. Those blooms with the bonfire reek
And the flaming of ruby, copper, gold —
There boyhood's sun foretold, retold
   A full gamut of setting and rising.

Something touched him. Always the scene
   Was to haunt his memory —
Not haunt — come alive there, as if what had been
But a flowery idea took flesh in the womb
Of his solitude, rayed out a rare, real bloom.
   I know, for I was he.

And today, when I see chrysanthemums,
  I half envy that boy
For whom they spoke as muffled drums
Darkly messaging, 'All decays;
But youth's brief agony can blaze
  Into a posthumous joy.'

Song

Written to an Irish Air (Dermott)

Love was once light as air
Brushed over all my thoughts and themes;
Love once seemed kind as air
When the dewfall gleams.
Now he's another thing —
Naked light, oh hard to bear,
Too much discovering
With his noonday beams.

Long had I sought for you,
Long, long by subtle masks delayed:
Fair shapes I thought were you
On my green heart played.
Now love at his height informs
All that was so vague to view,
Shall not those slighter forms
In his noon hour fade?

Fade they then fast as snow
When April brings the earth to light,
One shape — alas 'tis so —
Still lingers white:

One heart-wrung phantom still,
One I would not tell to go,
Shadows my noontime still
And haunts my night.

On the Sea Wall

As I came to the sea wall that August day,
One out of all the bathers there
Beckoned my eye, a girl at play
With the surf-flowers. Was it the dark, dark hair
Falling Egyptian-wise, or the way
Her body curved to the spray? —

I know not. Only my heart was shaking
Within me, and then it stopped; as though
You were dead and your shape had returned to haunt me
On the very same spot where, five years ago,
You slipped from my arms and played in the breaking
Surges to tease and enchant me.

I could not call out. Had there been no more
Than those thickets of rusty wire to pen us
Apart, I'd have gone to that girl by the shore
Hoping she might be you. But between us
Lie tangled, severing, stronger far,
Barbed relics of love's old war.

Ewig

Multitudes of corn
Shock-still in July heat,
Year upon foaming year
Of may and meadowsweet —
Soon, soon they fleet.

So many words to unsay,
So much hue and cry
After a wisp of flame,
So many deaths to die
Ere the heart runs dry.

The Neurotic

The spring came round, and still he was not dead.
Skin of the earth deliciously powdered
With buttercups and daisies — oh, Proserpina
Refreshed by sleep, wild-cherry-garlanded
And laughing in the sallies of the willow-wren!
With lambs and lilies spring came round again.

Who would suppose, seeing him walk the meadows,
He walks a treadmill there, grinding himself
To powder, dust to greyer dust, or treads
An invisible causeway lipped by chuckling shadows?
Take his arm if you like, you'll not come near him.
His mouth is an ill-stitched wound opening: hear him.

'I will not lift mine eyes unto the hills
For there white lambs nuzzle and creep like maggots.
I will not breathe the lilies of the valley

For through their scent a chambered corpse exhales.
If a petal floats to earth, I am oppressed.
The grassblades twist, twist deep in my breast.'

The night came on, and he was still alive.
Lighted tanks of streets a-swarm with denizens
Darting to trysts, sauntering to parties.
How all the heart-fires twinkle! Yes, they thrive
In the large illusion of freedom, in love's net
Where even the murderer can act and the judge regret.

This man who turns a phrase and twiddles a glass
Seems far from that pale muttering magician
Pent in a vicious circle of dilemmas.
But could you lift his blue, thick gaze and pass
Behind, you would walk a stage where endlessly
Phantoms rehearse unactable tragedy.

'In free air captive, in full day benighted,
I am as one for ever out of his element
Transparently enwombed, who from a bathysphere
Observes, wistful, amazed, but more affrighted,
Gay fluent forms of life weaving around,
And dares not break the bubble and be drowned.'

His doomsdays crawled like lava, till at length
All impulse clogged, the last green lung consumed,
Each onward step required the sweat of nightmare,
Each human act a superhuman strength . . .
And the guillemot, clotted with oil, droops her head.
And the mouse between the elastic paws shams dead.

Death mask of a genius unborn:
Tragic prince of a rejected play:
Soul of suffering that bequeathed no myth:
A dark tower and a never-sounded horn. —
Call him what we will, words cannot ennoble
This Atlas who fell down under a bubble.

Seen from the Train

Somewhere between Crewkerne
And Yeovil it was. On the left of the line
Just as the crinkled hills unroll
To the plain. A church on a small green knoll —
A limestone church,
And above the church
Cedar boughs stretched like hands that yearn
To protect or to bless. The whole

Stood up, antique and clear
As a cameo, from the vale. I swear
It was not a dream. Twice, thrice had I found it
Chancing to look as my train wheeled round it.
But this time I passed,
Though I gazed as I passed
All the way down the valley, that knoll was not there,
Nor the church, nor the trees it mounded.

What came between to unsight me? . . .
But suppose, only suppose there might be
A secret look in a landscape's eye
Following you as you hasten by,
And you have your chance —
Two or three chances
At most — to hold and interpret it rightly,
Or it is gone for aye.

There was a time when men
Would have called it a vision, said that sin
Had blinded me since to a heavenly fact.
Well, I have neither invoked nor faked
Any church in the air,
And little I care
Whether or no I shall see it again.
But blindly my heart is racked

When I think how, not twice or thrice,
But year after year in another's eyes
I have caught the look that I missed today
Of the church, the knoll, the cedars — a ray
Of the faith, too, they stood for,
The hope they were food for,
The love they prayed for, facts beyond price —
And turned my eyes away.

Outside and In

How pretty it looks, thought a passer-by —
That cyclamen on her windowsill:
Flowers flushed like the butterfly kisses of sleep that
    illumine
A child's alabaster cheek.
She who set it there must have warm hopes to bloom in,
So happy it looks, thought the passer-by,
On the newcomer's windowsill.

O passer-by, can you not feel my glances
Beating against the pane,
Fluttering like a moth shut off from the glades of musk
And the moonlit dances?
O passer-by, can you not see it plain?

She comes not to meet us, muttered the neighbours
Peering in from the stony street:
But look at her parlour, all lighted and spider-spruce!
How saucily wink the brasses!
So garnished a room never tokens a pure recluse.
Let us hope she'll bring, said the gossiping neighbours,
No scandal upon our street.

Ah, what do you know of the crippled heart, my neighbours,
That shrinks from the light and the press?
My winking brass, all the fine repetitive web
Of my house-proud labours —
Even I dare not know them for signals of distress.

A happy release, murmured the living
As they carried at last out into the world
Her body, light as a bird's that has died of hunger
Beneath some warped hedgerow:
Though it was her own doing if all humanity shunned her,
Yet a happy release to be done with living
An outcast from the world.

O living hearts, you are wrong once more. Unassuaged
Even now are my pangs, my fears.
I starved amid plenty. Death seemed no deliverance
To flesh that was caged,
O living hearts, in a ghost these fifty years.

From An Italian Visit (1953)

To Henry Reed

*. . . an Italian visit is a voyage of discovery, not only
of scenes and cities, but also of the latent faculties of
the traveller's heart and mind . . .*
JASPER MORE: *The Land of Italy*

Part Two
Flight to Italy

The winged bull trundles to the wired perimeter.
Cumbrously turns. Shivers, brakes clamped,
Bellowing four times, each engine tested
With routine ritual. Advances to the runway.
Halts again as if gathering heart
Or warily snuffing for picador cross-winds.
Then, then, a roar open-throated
Affronts the arena. Then fast, faster
Drawn by the magnet of his *idée fixe,*
Head down, tail up, he's charging the horizon.
   And the grass of the airfield grows smooth as a fur.
The runway's elastic and we the projectile;
Installations control-tower mechanics parked aeroplanes —
Units all woven to a ribbon unreeling,
Concrete melts and condenses to an abstract
Blur, and our blood thickens to think of
Rending, burning, as suburban terraces
Make for us, wave after wave.
                              The moment
Of Truth is here. We can only trust,
Being as wholly committed to other hands
As a babe at birth, Europa to the bull god.
And as when one dies in his sleep, there's no divining
The instant of take-off, so we who were earth-bound
Are air-borne, it seems, in the same breath.
The neutered terraces subside beneath us.

   Bank and turn, bank and turn,
Air-treading bull, my silver Alitalia!
Bank and turn, while the earth below
Swings like a dial on the wing-tip's axis,
Whirls and checks like a wheel of chance!

Now keep your course! On azure currents
Let the wings lift and sidle drowsily —
A halcyon rocked by the ghost of the gale.
To watchers in Kent you appear as a quicksilver
Bead skimming down the tilted sky;
To the mild-eyed aircrew, an everyday office:
To us, immured in motion, you mean
A warm womb pendant between two worlds.
        O trance prenatal and angelic transport!
Like embryos curled in this aluminium belly —
Food and oxygen gratis — again
We taste the pure freedom of the purely submissive,
The passive dominion of the wholly dependent.
Through heaven's transparent mysteries we travel
With a humdrum of engines, the mother's heartbeat:
And our foreshadowed selves begin to take shape, to be
Dimly adapted to their destination.
What migrant fancies this journeying generates! —
Almost we imagine a metempsychosis.

        Over the Channel now, beneath the enchanting
Inane babble of a baby-blue sky,
We soar through cloudland, at the heights of nonsense.
From a distance they might be sifted-sugar-drifts,
Meringues, iced cakes, confections of whipped cream
Lavishly piled for some Olympian party —
A child's idea of heaven. Now radiant
All around the airscrew's boring penumbra
The clouds redouble, as nearer we climb,
Their toppling fantasy. We skirt the fringe of icebergs,
Dive under eiderdowns, disport with snowmen
On fields of melting snow dinted by the wind's feet,
Gleefully brush past atom-bomb cauliflowers,
Frozen fluffs of spray from naval gunfire.
        Wool-gathering we fly through a world of make-believe.
We *are* the aircraft, the humming-bird hawk moth
Hovering and sipping at each cloud corolla;
But also ourselves, to whom these white follies are

Valid as symbols for a tonic reverie
Or as symptoms of febrile flight from the real.
Let us keep, while we can, the holiday illusion,
The heart's altimeter dancing bliss-high,
Forgetting gravity, regardless of earth
Out of sight, out of mind, like a menacing letter
Left at home in a drawer — let the next-of-kin
　　acknowledge it.

　　　The cloud-floor is fissured suddenly. Clairvoyance
It seems, not sight, when the solid air frays and parts
Unveiling, like some rendezvous remote in a crystal,
Bright, infinitesimal, a fragment of France.
We scan the naked earth as it were through a skylight:
Down there, what life-size encounters, what industrious
Movement and vocations manifold go forward!
But to us, irresponsible, above the battle,
Villages and countryside reveal no more life than
A civilization asleep beneath a glacier,
Toy bricks abandoned on a plain of linoleum . . .
　　　After a hard winter, on the first warm day
The invalid venturing out into the rock-garden,
Pale as a shaft of December sunshine, pauses,
All at sea among the aubrietia, the alyssum
And arabis — halts and moves on how warily,
As if to take soundings where the blossom foams and
　　tumbles:
But what he does sound is the depth of his own weakness
At last, as never when pain-storms lashed him.
So we, convalescent from routine's long fever,
Plummeting our gaze down to river and plain,
Question if indeed that dazzling world beneath us
Be truth or delirium; and finding still so tentative
The answer, can gauge how nearly we were ghosts,
How far we must travel yet to flesh and blood.

　　　But now the engines have quickened their beat
And the fuselage pulsates, panting like a fugitive.

Below us — oh, look at it! — earth has become
Sky, a thunderscape curdling to indigo,
Veined with valleys of green fork-lightning.
The atrocious Alps are upon us. Their ambush —
A primeval huddle, then a bristling and heaving of
Brutal boulder-shapes, an uprush of Calibans —
Unmasks its white-fanged malice to maul us.
The cabin grows colder. Keep height, my angel!
Where we are, all but terra firma is safe.
      Recall how flyers from a raid returning,
Lightened of one death, were elected for another:
Their homing thoughts too far ahead, a mountain
Stepped from the mist and slapped them down.
We, though trivial the hazard, retract
Our trailing dreams until we have cleared these ranges.
Exalted, numinous, aloof no doubt
To the land-locked vision, for us they invoke
A mood more intimate, a momentary flutter and
Draught of danger — death's fan coquettishly
Tapping the cheek ere she turn to dance elsewhere.
Our mien is the bolder for this mild flirtation,
Our eyes the brighter, since every brush with her
Gives flesh a souvenir, a feel of resurrection.

      Those peaks o'erpassed, we glissade at last to
A gentian pasture, the Genoan sea.
Look south, sky-goers! In flying colours
A map's unrolled there — the Italy
Your schooldays scanned once: the hills are sand-blond,
A pale green stands for the littoral plain:
The sea's bedizened with opening islands
Like iris eyes on a peacock's fan.
How slowly dawns on the drowsy newborn
Whose world's unworn yet — a firelit dress,
An ego's glamorous shell, a womb of rumours —
The first faint glimmering of otherness!
But half awake, we could take this country
For some vague drift from prenatal dreams:

Those hills and headlands, like sleep's projections
Or recollections, mere symbol seem.
        Then hurtling southward along shores of myrtle,
Silverly circle the last lap,
My bull-headed moth! This land is nothing
But a mythical name on an outline map
For us, till we've scaled it to our will's dimensions,
Filled in each wayward, imperious route,
Shaded it in with delays and chagrins,
Traced our selves over it, foot by foot.
Now tighter we circle, as if the vertical
Air is a whirlpool drawing us down;
And the airfield, a candle-bright pinpoint, invites us
To dance ere alighting . . . Hurry! We burn
For Rome so near us, for the phoenix moment
When we have thrown off this traveller's trance,
And mother-naked and ageless-ancient
Wake in her warm nest of renaissance.

Part Three

A Letter from Rome

We have been here three days, and Rome is really —
I know, I know; it would take three life-times to cover
The glorious junk-heap. Besides, our generation —
Well, you've only to think of James, as one must do here,
Lapping the cream of antiquity, purring over
Each vista that stroked his senses, and in brief
Rubbing himself against Rome like a great tabby,
To see what I mean. We who 'flowered' in the Thirties
Were an odd lot; sceptical yet susceptible,
Dour though enthusiastic, horizon-addicts

And future-fans, terribly apt to ask what
Our all-very-fine sensations were in aid of.
We did not, you will remember, come to coo.
Still, there is hope for us. Rome has absorbed
Other barbarians: yes, and there's nobody quite so
Sensuously rich and reckless as the reformed
Puritan . . . This by the way, to establish a viewpoint.
       You wanted my impressions. If only one were
A simple sieve, be the mesh close or wide,
For Rome to shake (and how it does shake one!), sifting
Some finer stuff from the coarser. But the trouble with me is
— Or perhaps it's the trouble with Rome — to discriminate
Merely between what is here and what has been here,
Between the eye and the mind's eye. The place has had
Over two thousand years of advance publicity
For us, which clouds the taste and saps the judgment.
What are you to do when Catullus buttonholes you
On the way to St. Peter's? When the Colosseum presents
Nero[1] comparing notes with Roderick Hudson
On art and egotism? Sights, sounds, phantoms —
It is all too much for me, it should not be allowed!
       Perhaps, though, it is just here that something emerges.
As when, composing a poem, the tangle of images
And jangle of words pressing hard on you, mobbing you, may
Compel you to choose the right moment to disengage
And find the one word, the word of command which makes
     them
Meekly fall in to their ranks, and the march continues:
So from this Rome, where the past lies weltering
In the blood of the present, and posters of Betty Grable
Affront the ghost of Cato; from all its grandiose
Culs-de-sac — the monumental gateways
That open on nothing, the staircases starting for heaven,
The stone-blind palaces sweltering in the noon;
From the stilled tempest of the Sistine ceiling
To the water exasperated by sirocco

---

[1] The Colosseum was built by Vespasian on the site of the Golden House of Nero.

In every fountain basin; from the whole gamut,
Theatrical, vulgar, rhetorical, fractious, sublime,
Of a city young as Tithonus, a city so ancient
That even the shadows here lie thick as dust: —
Emerges from all this, like invisible writing
Drawn out by the heart's warmth, one lucid word.

      Compost. I do not suppose the word original
(Original! Rome is quite beyond that). But think of it —
Century into century rotting down,
Faith piled on faith, Mithra on Jupiter,
Christ upon Mithra, Catholicism on Christ,
Temples imbedded in churches, church-stones in palaces:
Think of the pagan gods, demoted to demons,
Haunting and taunting the Early Fathers; long-dead
Lights of love, immortalized as Madonnas,
Demurely smiling at man's infant idealism.
Superstition, sanctity, cruelty, laws, art, lust —
Layer after layer laid down, course upon course
They renew the soul of this city, a city whose prospects
Are quarried out of its bones, a soul digesting
All foreignness into one rich dark fibre.
Rome, I can tell you, is the very type of
The hugger-mugger of human growth. For here
You can see the grand design eternally crossed
By the abject means, and its seedy ruin redeemed with
Valerian, arbutus, fennel; a character root-fast
Like a man's in the deposit of all his acts.

      Or say, a woman's; for so she appeared to us
On the first morning when we sauntered out
(The night before, wild strawberries and Frascati
Gold as the Roman May-light, cool as grottoes).
A woman — how shall I put it? — who makes you feel
She has waited two thousand years to meet you, and now
At once she is wholly yours, her liquid tongue,
Her body mantled in the full flush of Ceres,
And Primavera fluttering in her eyes.
She can be tiresome, no doubt, feverish, languid,
Changing her moods like dresses. But today

She has chosen to be divinely acquiescent:
'What shall we do?' the shell-like murmur comes,
'Shall we go shopping? Would you like me to show you the
    sights?
'I will do anything you say, anything.'
. . . So we took, in the end, a carrozza to St. Peter's.
The driver was plainly a phantom; his conveyance
Jarred like old bones and mumbled of better days when
Violet-adorned beauties, sedate or giddy,
Turned all heads on the Corso. Thus we went
Jaunting over the seven hills of Rome
With the streets rocking beneath us as if seven ages
Turned in their grave, while noise upon noise the drift
Of our own — its voices, horns, wheels, bells, loudspeakers —
Washed past us; then it dwindled away to a sea-shell
Cadence, beyond the Tiber, as we came near
Vatican city.

        And now *vates tacete*
Should be the word. Words here can only scrabble
Like insects at the plinth of a colossus,
Scrabble and feebly gesticulate and go elsewhere.
Mere magnitude one might deal with, or pure and simple
Meaning; but both in one, they give no purchase.
A dome superb as heaven's vault, capping a story
Whose hero blessed the meek; a desert of floor
Refracting faith like a mirage; the orchestration
Of gold and marble engulfing the still, small voice: —
You cannot pass over St. Peter's and what it stands for,
Whether you see it as God's vicarious throne
Or the biggest bubble ever yet unpricked.
And here, I have to confess, the old Puritan peeped out;
Not in sour protest against the Scarlet Woman,
Nor quite in the mood of my generation — its volatile
Mixture of hero-worship and disrespect;
But that an early habit of going to church
Prevents me from going to churches, however distinguished
Their provenance, just as a sight-seer. Faith perhaps,

Though unconscious, is not yet dead, its breath still clouding
The glass of aesthetic perception. Apart from which,
I could not do with the guides who spring up like sweat-white
Fungi from every chink, and cling to one, furtively
Offering their curious knowledge; these pimps are not
The type you would choose to lead you to any altar.
So I was lost, ill at ease here, until by chance
In a side chapel we found a woman mourning
Her son: all the *lacrimae rerum* flowed
To her gesture of grief, all life's blood from his stone.
There is no gap or discord between the divine
And the human in that pietà of Michelangelo.
Then, after a marathon walk through the Vatican galleries,
An endless belt of statues, tapestry, pictures
Glazing the eye, we came out into the streets again.
Better than all the museums, this strolling folk
Who sun themselves in the apricot light of antiquity
And take its prestige for granted. Cameo faces,
Contessa or contadina; bronze boys skylarking
As if they had just wriggled free from a sculptor's hand —
How easily art and nature overlap here!
Another thing you would like about the Romans
Is the way they use their city, not as a warren
Of bolt-holes, nor a machine into which one is fed
Each morning and at evening duly disgorged,
But as an open-air stage. Palazzo, tenement
Seem pure façade — back-cloth for a continuous
Performance of business, love-making, politics, idling,
Conducted with a grand operatic extravagance
At the tempo of family theatricals. That same night
In the Piazza dell' Esedra, sipping
Grappa, we watched the people, warm as animals
And voluble as fountains, eddying round
While the floodlit masonry was mere slabs of moonshine.
Rome is a city where flesh and blood can never
Be sacrificed, or mistaken, for abstractions.
        But already (you can imagine how) my mind's
Crisscrossed with figures, memoranda, lightning sketches,

Symbolic doodlings, hour by hour set down
Haphazardly as in Rome era on era.
And time is already shuffling tricks with discards.
Those fountains yesterday at the Villa d'Este
Grouped like patrician spectres in white conclave
Against a drop-scene of terraces and urns —
Did we indeed see them, or have they stepped
From a picture book years ago perused? Last night
We found on a wall of the Pincio a bas-relief,
A wide white calm imperious head suddenly
Surveying us out of the blank wall like some racial
Memory still not deep enough bricked up.

      Yesterday, then, was a day with the dead. We hired
A car, and set out first for the Palatine hill.
The Forum? Well, picture a clearing found
In the depth of a clamorous forest, a low space littered
With bits of temples, arches, altars, mosaics
And God knows what — classical tags, fag ends,
Smatterings and stumps of a once apparently stable
Civilization, which packed up for all that
And left, like a gipsy encampment or picnic party:
And over it all, the silence of sheer exhaustion.
This area, sad as scar-tissue now, was the heart
Of a great republic, the S.P.Q.R.
Here they governed — a people, like the Scots,
Smouldering, pious, intolerant, living hard,
And demon fighters. Warlike was the seed;
But Time has pushed out this crop of decayed teeth.
It was the usual story. Long before
Their aqueducts ran dry and became picturesque,
Their virtue had imperceptibly seeped away
Into the dunes of ambition. They caught
Luxury, like a syphilis, from their conquests.
Then, feeling queer, they appointed one man to cure them
And made a god of him. The disease was arrested
From time to time. But injections grew more frequent,
And the extremities began to rot;
While at home no amount of marble could hide the sick core —

Vestals too free with their flame, tribunes long impotent,
A rabble who had not the wherewithal to redeem its
Too often pledged heirlooms, justice and hardiness.
         So we were glad on the whole to leave this spot
Where glum mementoes of decline and fall
Are cherished like a grievance in Rome's heart,
And drive out towards Tivoli. The name
Had a certain frivolous charm for one oppressed
By dwelling on ruined greatness. The little town,
Modishly perched on an olive-tressed hillside,
Is famous for its sulphur springs (our driver
Stopped the car so that we might inhale it)
And of course, for the Villa d'Este. There at first
In the elaborate Renaissance gardens
Laid out for the lust of the eye, you seem to see
The lineaments of gratified desire.
An illusion though, like the smile on a dead face
Which means nothing but our own wish for peace.
Exquisite, yes: but a sense of the past, to be truly
Felicitous, demands some belief in the present,
Some moral belvedere we have not got.
This villa inhabited only by frescoes,
This garden groomed for sightseers — they mirror
Too clearly our lack of prospect or tenable premise.
The cardinals and princes who adorned them,
Lords of an age when men believed in man,
Are as remote from us as the Colosseum
Where high-tiered beasts howled down professional heroes;
Perhaps — it is a comfortless thought — remoter.
         Back, then, to Rome. At Tivoli our driver
Stopped again like some house-proud, indelicate devil
To remark the smell of sulphur. Presently,
Held in a crook of Rome's old city wall
Close by St. Paul's gate under the pagan shadow
Of Gaius Cestius' pyramid, we found
The English cemetery. An ox-eyed, pregnant,
Slatternly girl opened the gate for us
And showed us round the desirable estate.

Here is one corner of a foreign field
That is for ever garden suburb. See,
In their detached and smug-lawned residences,
Behind a gauze of dusty shrubs, the English
Indulge their life-long taste for privacy.
Garish Campagna knocks at the back door,
Rome calls *en grande tenue*: but 'not at home'
Murmur these tombs, and 'far from home they died,
'The eccentric couple you have come to visit —
'One spitting blood, an outsider and a failure,
'One sailing a boat, his mind on higher things.'
Somewhere close to the pyramid a loud-speaker
Blared jazz while we lingered at Keats' shabby mound,
But the air was drowned by the ghost of a nightingale;
The ground was swimming with anemone tears
Where Shelley lay.
                    We could feel at home here, with
This family of exiles. It is our people:
A people from whose reticent, stiff heart
Babble the springtime voices, always such voices
Bubbling out of their clay . . .
                            So much for Rome.
Tomorrow we shall take the bus to Florence.

Part Four

Bus to Florence

In the white piazza Today is barely awake.
      A well-water breeze freshens
Her nakedness, musky with love, and wafts about
      Her breath of moist carnations.
Oh the beautiful creature, still in a dream pinioned,
      A flutter of meadowsweet thighs!

How she clings to the night, whose fingertips haunt her
      waxen
      Body! Look at the eyes
Opening — pale, drenched, languid as aquamarines!
      They are open. The mere-smooth light
Starts glancing all over the city in jets and sparklets
      Like a charm of goldfinches in flight.
The tousled alleys stretch. Tall windows blink.
      Hour of alarum clocks and laces.
Sprinklers dust off the streets. The shops hum gently
      As they make up their morning faces.
And today comes out like a bride, a different woman,
      Subtler in hue, hazier,
Until the pensive mist goes, shyly avowing
      Such a zenith of shameless azure.

      This is our day: we mean
To make much of her, tune to her pitch. The enchanting
      creature
      Travels with us. For once
There will be no twinge of parting in a departure.
      So eager she is to be off,
Spilling her armful of roses and mignonette,
      Her light feet restlessly echoed
From campanile and wristwatch (will they forget?
      Be late?) What a stir and lustre
Ripple the white square at a lift of her hand!
      Look! she has seen us, she points to
That blue bus with the scarab-like trailer behind.

We went the Cassian Way, a route for legions,
      We and the May morning.
Rome flaked off in stucco; blear-eyed villas
      Melancholiac under their awnings.
Rome peeled off like a cataract. Clear beyond us
      A vision good to believe in —
The Campagna with its longdrawn sighs of grass
      Heaving, heaving to heaven.

This young-old terrain of asphodel and tufo
    Opening its heart to the sun,
Was it sighing for death like Tithonus, or still athirst for
    Immortal dews? . . . We run
Towards Tuscany now through a no-man's-land where
    stilted
    Aqueducts dryly scale
The distance and sport the lizard his antediluvian
    Head and tendril tail.
But soon the road rivers between flowerbanks:
    Such a fume and flamboyance of purple
Vetch, of campions, poppy, wild rose, gladioli,
    Bugloss! The flowery people,
Come out in their best to line our route, how they wave
    At the carnival progress! And higher,
The foothills flush with sanfoin, salutes of broom
    Are setting the rocks on fire.
Sutri, Viterbo, Montefiascone passed:
    Each village, it seemed, was making
A silent bar in the music, the road's hurdy-gurdy
    Winding, the tambourine shaking
Of sunlit leaves. You tatterdemalion townships —
    Elegance freaked with decay —
Your shuttered looks and your black doormouths gaping
    Dumb in the heat of the day
Reject, unanswered, the engine's urgent beat.
    But now, groves of acacia
Swing their honeybells peal upon peal to welcome us
    Over the vibrant, azure,
Deep organ chords of Bolsena, the silvery wavelets
    Trilling tranquillamente.
That music followed us for miles, until
    We came to Acquapendente.

Eyes grown used to the light, we were finding our form and
    meeting
    Impressions squarely.
Yet, where all was new, changeful, idyllic, it saddened

> To think how rarely
More than a few snippets remain from the offered fabric,
> And they not always
The ones we'd have chosen. It's sequence I lack, the talent
> to grasp
> Not a here-and-there phrase
But the music entire, its original stream and logic. I'd better
> Accept this, perhaps,
As nature's way: matter, the physicists tell one, is largely
> A matter of gaps.

Another stage, and a change of key. Listen!
> Rosetted oxen move —
The milky skins, the loose-kneed watersilk gait of
> Priestesses vowed to Love.
A road stubborn with stone pines. Shrines at the roadside.
> A sandstone cliff, where caves
Open divining mouths: in this or that one
> A skeleton sibyl raves.
Signs and omens . . . We approached the haunts of
> The mystery-loving Etruscans.
Earth's face grew rapidly older, ravine-wrinkled,
> Shadowed with brooding dusk on
Temple and cheek. Mountains multiplied round us
> And the flowery guise shredded off as we
Climbed past boulders and gaunt grass high into
> A landscape haggard as prophecy,
Scarred with bone-white riverbeds like veins
> Of inspiration run dry.
Still what a journey away the apocalypse! See it —
> A tower, a town in the sky!
A child from the flowering vale, a youth from the foothills
> May catch glimpses of death
Remote as a star, irrelevant, all of a lifetime
> Ahead, less landmark than myth.
For ages it seems no nearer. But imperceptibly
> The road, twisting and doubling
As if to delay or avoid it, underlines

That Presence: the man is troubled,
Feeling the road beneath him being hauled in now
        Like slack, the magnetic power
Of what it had always led to over the dreaming
        Hills and the fable of flowers.
So, while the bus toiled upwards and the Apennines
        Swirled like vapours about it,
That town in the sky stayed constant and loomed nearer
        Till we could no more doubt it;
And soon, though still afar off, it darkly foretold us
        We were destined to pass that way.
We passed by the thundercloud castle of Radicofani
        At the pinnacle of our day.

The wrack of cloud, the surly ruinous tower
Stubborn upon the verge of recognition —
        What haunts and weights them so?
        Memory, or premonition?
Why should a mouldering finger in the sky,
An hour of cloud that drifts and passes, mean
        More than the flowering vale,
        The volcanic ravine?
A driven heart, a raven-shadowing mind
Loom above all my pastorals, impend
        My traveller's joy with fears
        That travelling has no end.

But on without pause from that eyrie the bus, swooping,
        Checking and swooping, descends:
The road cascades down the hillface in blonde ringlets
        Looped up with hairpin bends.
The sun rides out. The calcined earth grows mellow
        With place-names sleek as oil —
Montepulciano, Montalcino, Murlo,
        Castiglione. The soil
Acknowledges man again, his hand which husbands
        Each yielding inch and endures
To set the vine amid armies, the olive between

Death's adamantine spurs.
Presently, on a constellation of three hills,
    We saw crowning the plain
A town from a missal, a huddle of towers and houses,
    Mediaeval Siena.
A gorge of a street, anfractuous, narrow. Our bus
    Crawled up it, stemming a torrent
Of faces — the faces impetuous, proud, intransigent
    Of those who had fought with Florence
For Tuscany. Was it a demonstration they flocked to?
    A miracle? Or some huger
Event? We left the bus stranded amongst them, a monster
    Thrown up from their fathomless future,
And strolled into a far-off present, an age
    Where all is emblematic,
Pure, and without perspective. The twining passages,
    Diagrams of some classic
Doctrinal knot, lap over and under one another.
    The swan-necked Mangia tower
With its ruff stands, clear as Babel, for pride: beneath it,
    Shaped like a scallop, that square
Might be humility's dewpond, or the rose-madder
    Shell from which Aphrodite
Once stepped ashore. And the west front of the Duomo —
    How it images, flight upon flight, the
Ascending torrent, a multitude without number
    Intent on their timeless way
From the world of St. Catherine, Boccaccio and Fiammetta
    Towards the judgment day!

A township cast up high and dry from an age
    When the whole universe
    Of stars lived in man's parish
And the zodiac told his fortune, chapter and verse.
A simple time — salvation or damnation
    One black and white device,
    Eternity foreshortened,

Earth a mere trusting step from Paradise.
O life where mystery grew on every bush,
    Saints, tyrants, thrills and throes
    Were for one end! — the traveller
Dips into your dream and, sighing, goes.

After two hours we went on, for our destination
    Called. The adagio dance
Of olives, their immemorial routine and eccentric
    Variations of stance;
The vines that flourished like semaphore alphabets endlessly
    Flagging from hill to hill:
We knew them by heart now (or never would), seeing them
    tiny
    And common as tormentil.
Florence invisibly haled us. The intervening
    Grew misted with expectations,
Diminished yet weirdly prolonged, as all the go-between
    World by a lover's impatience.
Through Poggibonsi we glided — a clown's name
    And a history of hard knocks:
But nothing was real till at length we entered the nonpareil
    City . . . A hand unlocks
The traveller's trance. We alight. And the just coming down
    to
    Earth, the pure sense of arrival,
More than visions or masterpieces, fulfil
    One need for which we travel.

    This day, my bride of a day,
Went with me hand in hand the centuried road:
    I through her charmed eyes gazing,
She hanging on my words, peace overflowed.
    But now, a rose-gold Eve,
With the deep look of one who will unbosom
    Her sweetest to death only,
She opens out, she flames and falls like blossom.

A spray that lightly trembles
After the warbler's flown. A cloud vibrating
In the wash of the hull-down sun.
My heart rocks on. Remembering, or awaiting?

Part Six

Elegy Before Death: At Settignano

(To R.N.L.)
. . . for be it never so derke
Me thinketh I see hir ever mo.
CHAUCER

Come to the orangery. Sit down awhile.
The sun is setting: the veranda frames
An illuminated leaf of Italy.
Gold and green and blue, stroke upon stroke,
Seem to tell what nature and man could make of it
If only their marriage were made in heaven. But see,
Even as we hold the picture,
The colours are fading already, the lines collapsing
Fainting into the dream they will soon be.

Again? Again we are baffled who have sought
So long in a melting Now the formula
Of Always. There is no fast dye. Always? —
That is the word the sirens sing
On bone island. Oh stop your ears, and stop
All this vain peering through the haze,
The fortunate haze wherein we change and ripen,
And never mind for what. Let us even embrace
The shadows wheeling away our windfall days.

Again again again, the frogs are screeling
Down by the lilypond. Listen! I'll echo them —
Gain gain gain . . . Could we compel
One grain of one vanishing moment to deliver
Its golden ghost, loss would be gain
And Love step naked from illusion's shell.
Did we but dare to see it,
All things to us, you and I to each other,
Stand in this naked potency of farewell.

The villa was built for permanence. Man laid down
Like wine his heart, planted young trees, young pictures,
Young thoughts to ripen for an heir.
Look how these avenues take the long view
Of things ephemeral! With what aplomb
The statues greet us at the grassy stair!
Time on the sundial was a snail's migration
Over a world of warmth, and each day passing
Left on the fertile heart another layer.

The continuity they took for granted
We wistfully glamourize. So life's devalued:
Worth not a rhyme
These statues, groves, books, bibelots, masterpieces,
If we have used them only to grout a shaken
Confidence or stop up the gaps of time.
We must ride the flood, or go under
With all our works, to emerge, when it recedes,
Derelicts sluggish from the dishonouring slime.

Our sun is setting. Terrestrial planes shift
And slide towards dissolution, the terraced gardens
Quaver like waves, and in the garden urn
Geraniums go ashen. Now are we tempted, each
To yearn that his struggling counterpoint, carried away
Drowned by the flood's finale, shall return
To silence. Why do we trouble
A master theme with cadenzas
That ring out, fade out over its fathomless unconcern?

Love, more than our holidays are numbered.
Not one day but a whole life is drained off
Through this pinprick of doubt into the dark.
Rhadamanthine moment! Shall we be judged
Self-traitors? Now is a chance to make our flux
Stand and deliver its holy spark, —
Now, when the tears rise and the levees crumble,
To tap the potency of farewell.
What ark is there but love? Let us embark.

A weeping firmament, a sac of waters,
A passive chaos — time without wind or tide,
Where on brief motiveless eddy seethe
Lost faces, furniture, animals, oblivion's litter —
Envelop me, just as the incipient poem
Is globed in nescience, and beneath
A heart purged of all but memory, grows.
No landfall yet? No rift in the film? . . . I send you
My dove into the future, to your death.

*

A dove went forth: flits back a ghost to me,
Image of her I imagine lost to me,
Up the road through Fiesole we first travelled on —
Was it a week or thirty years ago?
Time vanishes now like a mirage of water,
Touched by her feet returning whence she had gone,
Touched by the tones that darkly appeal to me,
The memories that make her shade as real to me
As all the millions breathing under the upright sun.

We are back at the first time we went abroad together.
Homing to this garden with a love-sure bent
Her phantom has come. Now hand in hand we stray
Through a long-ago morning mounting from a lather
Of azaleas and dizzy with the lemon blossom's scent.

And I seem to hear her murmur in the old romantic way,
'So blissfully, rosily our twin hearts burn here,
'This vernal time, whenever we return here,
'To haunter and haunted will be but yesterday.'

I follow her wraith down the terraced gardens
Through a dawn of nightingales, a murmurous siesta,
By leaf-green frogs on lily leaves screeling again
Towards eve. Is it dark or light? Fireflies glister
Across my noon, and nightlong the cicadas
Whir like a mechanical arm scratching in the brain.
All yesterday's children who fleetingly caressed her
Break ranks, break time, once more to join and part us:
I alone, who possessed her, feel the drag of time's harsh
    chain.

'Ah, you,' she whispers; 'are you still harping
'On mortal delusion? still the too much hoping
'Who needs only plant an acorn to dream a dryad's kiss?
'Still the doubtful one who, when she came to you
'Out of the rough rind, a naked flame for you,
'Fancied some knot or flaw in love, something amiss?'
Yes, such I am. But since I have found her
A revenant so fleshed in my memories, I wonder
Is she the real one and am I a wisp from the abyss.

Dare I follow her through the wood of obscurity —
This ilex grove where shades are lost in shade?
Not a gleam here, nothing differs, nothing sings, nothing
    grows,
For the trees are columns which ebonly support
A crypt of hollow silence, a subliminal thought,
A theorem proving the maggot equivalent to the rose.
Undiminished she moves here, shines, and will not fade.
Death, what had she to do with your futile purity,
The dogma of bone that on rare and common you would
    impose?

Her orbit clasped and enhanced in its diadem
All creatures. Once on a living night
When cypresses jetted like fountains of wine-warm air
Bubbling with fireflies, we going outside
In the palpitating dark to admire them,
One of the fireflies pinned itself to her hair;
And its throbbings, I thought, had a tenderer light
As if some glimmering of love inspired them,
As if her luminous heart was beating there.

Ah, could I make you see this subtle ghost of mine,
Delicate as a whorled shell that whispers to the tide,
Moving with a wavering watersilk grace,
Anemone-fingered, coral-tinted, under whose crystalline
Calm such naiads, angel fish and monsters sleep or slide;
If you could see her as she flows to me apace
Through waves through walls through time's fine mesh
        magically drawn,
You would say, this was surely the last daughter of the
        foam-born,
One whom no age to come will ever replace.

Eve's last fainting rose cloud; mornings that restored her
With orange tree, lemon tree, lotus, bougainvillea:
The milk-white snake uncoiling and the flute's light-fingered
        charm:
Breast of consolation, tongue of tried acquaintance:
A tranquil mien, but under it the nervous marauder
Slithering from covert, a catspaw from a calm:
Heaven's city adored in the palm of a pictured saint:
My vision's *ara coeli*, my lust's familiar,
All hours, moods, shapes, desires that yield, elude, disarm —

All woman she was. Brutalizing, humanizing,
Pure flame, lewd earth was she, imperative as air
And weak as water, yes all women to me.
To the rest, one of many, though they felt how she was rare
In sympathy and tasted in her warm words a sweetness

Of life that has ripened on the sunny side of the tree.
To herself a darker story, as she called her past to witness —
A heart much bruised, how often, how stormily surmising
Some chasmal flaw divided it from whole felicity.

So I bless the villa on the hill above Fiesole,
For here and now was flawless, and the past could not
      encroach
On its charmed circle to menace or to taunt her.
Oh, time that clung round her in unfading drapery,
Oh, land she wore like an enamelled brooch,
It was for remembrance you thus adorned her!
Now as I look back, how vividly, how gracefully
Ghosting there, she breathes me not the ghost of a
      reproach.
Happiness, it seems, can be the best haunter.

You later ones, should you see that wraith divulged for a
      moment
Through the sleep-haze of plumbago, glancing out from the
      loggia's
Vain dream of permanence as from a page
Time is already turning again, will you thus comment? —
'She is some dead beauty, no doubt, who queened here
      awhile
'And clasped her bouquets, and shrinks to leave the lighted
      stage:
'Not quite of the villa's classic period, though —
'Something more wistful, ironic, unstable in act and style,
'A minor masterpiece of a silver age.'

But to me she stands out tall as the Torcello madonna
Against a mosaic of sunlight, for ever upholding
My small, redeeming love. But 'love is all',
She says; and the mortal scene of planets and tides,
Animals, grass and men is transformed, proved, steadied
      around me.
But her I begin to view through a thickening veil,
A gauze of tears, till the figure inscrutably fades —

As every vision must vanish, if we and it keep faith,
Into the racked, unappeasable flesh of the real.

* * *

But look, the garden storm is stilled, the flood
Blinked away like a tear, earth reconciled to
Her molten birth-bed's long prophetic throes!
Her hills are lizards in their solid trance
Of sun and stone: upon each hill
Vine and olive hold the archaic pose:
Below, the bubble dome looks everlasting
As heaven's womb, and threading the eyes of bridges
Arno endlessly into the loom of oblivion flows.

A ghost, the mere thought of a shade, has done it.
Testing the shifty face of the Now with a dove, I found
Terra firma. Whatever in me was born to praise
Life's heart of blood or stone here reached its zenith,
Conjuring, staying, measuring all by that meek shade . . .
Now, love, you have tried on your phantom dress,
Return to nakedness!
Be breathing again beside me, real, imperfect!
Enmesh, enact my dream till it vanishes!

The oranges are going out? Tomorrow
Will light them up again. Tomorrow will call you
With nightingales; tomorrow will leave
A rose by your plate, and freshen the plumbago's
Blue millinery and open a parasol
Of cedar for you, as it did for the first, ignorant Eve
Before exile or death was thought of. But we know well
On what tenure we have this garden. Each day's a livelier
Paradise when each dawn is a reprieve.

I imagine you really gone for ever. Clocks stop.
Clouds bleed. Flames numb. My world shrunk to an echoing
Memorial skull. (A child playing at hide-

And-seek suddenly feels the whole terrible truth of
    Absence.)
Too keen the imagined grief, too dearly gained
Its proof of love. I would let all else slide,
Dissolve and perish into the old enigma,
If that could keep you here, if it could keep
Even your sad ghost at my side.

But gold and green and blue still glows before us
This leaf of Italy, the colours fixed
The characters formed by love. It is love's way
To shine most through the slow dusk of adieu.
Long may it glow within us, that timeless, halcyon halt
On our rough journey back to clay.
Oh, may my farewell word, may this your elegy
Written in life blood from a condemned heart
Be quick and haunting even beyond our day.

*   *   *

From Pegasus and Other Poems (1957)

To Jill

Pegasus

(In Memoriam: L.B.L.)

It was there on the hillside, no tall traveller's story.
A cloud caught on a whin-bush, an airing of bleached
Linen, a swan, the cliff of a marble quarry —
It could have been any of these: but as he approached,
He saw that it was indeed what he had cause
Both to doubt and believe in — a horse, a winged white
     horse.

It filled the pasture with essence of solitude.
The wind tiptoed away like an interloper,
The sunlight there became a transparent hood
Estranging what it revealed; and the bold horse-coper,
The invincible hero, trudging up Helicon,
Knew he had never before been truly alone.

It stood there, solid as ivory, dreamy as smoke;
Or moved, and its hooves went dewdropping so lightly
That even the wild cyclamen were not broken:
But when those hooves struck rock, such was their might
They tapped a crystal vein which flowed into song
As it ran through thyme and grasses down-along.

'Pegasus,' he called, 'Pegasus' — with the surprise
Of one for the first time naming his naked lover.
The creature turned its lordly, incurious eyes
Upon the young man; but they seemed to pass him over
As something beneath their pride or beyond their ken.
It returned to cropping the violets and cyclamen.

Such meekness, indifference frightened him more than any
Rumoured Chimaera. He wavered, remembering how
This milk-white beast was born from the blood of uncanny

198

Medusa, the nightmare-eyed: and at once, although
Its brief glance had been mild, he felt a cringing
And pinched himself to make sure he was not changing

Into a stone. The animal tossed its head;
The white mane lifted and fell like an arrogant whinny.
'Horses are meant to be ridden,' the hero said,
'Wings or no wings, and men to mount them. Athene
'Ordered my mission, besides, and certainly you
'Must obey that goddess,' he cried, and flung the lassoo.

The cyclamen bow their heads, the cicadas pause.
The mountain shivers from flank to snowy top,
Shaking off eagles as a pastured horse
Shakes off a cloud of flies. The faint airs drop.
Pegasus, with a movement of light on water,
Shimmers aside, is elsewhere, mocking the halter.

So there began the contest. A young man
Challenging, coaxing, pursuing, always pursuing
The dream of those dewfall hooves: a horse which ran
Quicksilver from his touch, sliding and slewing
Away, then immobile a moment, derisively tame,
Almost as if it entered into a game.

He summoned up his youth, his conscious art
To tire or trick the beast, criss-crossing the meadow
With a web of patient moves, circling apart,
Nearing, and pouncing, but only upon its shadow.
What skill and passion weave the subtle net!
But Pegasus goes free, unmounted yet.

All day he tried for this radiant creature. The more he
Persevered, the less he thought of the task
For which he required it, and the ultimate glory.
So it let him draw close, closer — nearly to grasp
Its mane; but that instant it broke out wings like a spread
Of canvas, and sailed off easily overhead.

He cursed Pegasus then. Anger arose
With a new desire, as if it were some white girl
To stretch, mount, master, exhaust in shuddering throes.
The animal gave him a different look: it swirled
Towards him, circled him round in a dazzling mist,
And one light hoof just knocked upon his breast.

The pale sky yawns to its uttermost concave,
Flowers open their eyes, rivulets prance
Again, and over the mountainside a wave
Of sparkling air tumbles. Now from its trance
That holy ground is deeply sighing and stirring.
The heights take back their eagles, cicadas are whirring.

The furious art, the pursuer's rhythmic pace
Failed in him now. Another self had awoken,
Which knew — but felt no chagrin, no disgrace —
That he, not the winged horse, was being broken:
It was his lode, his lord, his appointed star,
He but its shadow and familiar.

So he lay down to sleep. Argos, Chimaera,
Athene in one solution were immersed.
Around him, on bush and blade, each dewdrop mirrored
A star, his riding star, his universe,
While on the moonlit flowers at his side
Pegasus grazed, palpable, undenied.

A golden bridle came to him in sleep —
A mesh of immortal fire and sensual earth,
Pliant as love, compulsive as the sweep
Of light-years, brilliant as truth, perfect as death.
He dreamed a magic bridle, and next day
When he awoke, there to his hand it lay.

Wings furled, on printless feet through the dews of morn
Pegasus stepped, in majesty and submission,
Towards him. Mane of tempest, delicate mien,

It was all brides, all thoroughbreds, all pent passion.
Breathing flowers upon him, it arched a superb
Neck to receive the visionary curb.

Pegasus said, 'The bridle that you found
'In sleep, you yourself made. Your hard pursuit,
'Your game with me upon this hallowed ground
'Forged it, your failures tempered it. I am brute
'And angel. He alone, who taps the source
'Of both, can ride me. Bellerophon, I am yours.'

Psyche

He came to her that night, as every night,
Through the dark palace in a shape of darkness —
Or rather, it seemed to her, of light made invisible;
Came in a torrential swoop of feet
Or wings, and taking her filled her with sweetness:

Then slept, as the gods sleep who have no need
To dream. But she, awake in that dream palace
Where the wine poured itself and instruments played
At their own sweet will, began to feel afraid
That it was all some trick of the Love-Queen's malice.

A virgin once I roamed — my thoughts were vague
As a mother-of-pearl sky — before this beauty
Had grown to isolate me like a plague
From men, and set my sisters in jealous league.
It was I then who envied Aphrodite.

'Your husband,' they say, 'your husband is a dragon
'Sent to devour you.' And truly I am devoured
With love. But the daytimes drag, the tongues wag,
Distorting his unseen face; and I grow weak.
Can it be love that makes me such a coward?

Timidly then she touched his flank, which flowed
Like a river dreaming of rapids. Flesh it was,
Not scales. Each limb retraced was a midnight road
Humming with memories: each warm breath sighed
'Foolish girl, to believe only her eyes!'

Drowsing she closed her petals over this new
Delicate trust. But a quick remorse pierced her
That, doubting him, she had clouded her own love too;
And with it a seeming-pure desire to know
The facts of him who had so divinely possessed her.

Flesh of my flesh — yet between me and him
This maidenhead of dark. A voice, a stir,
A touch — no more, and yet my spirit's home.
Man, god, or fiend — blindly I worship him:
But he will tire of a blind worshipper.

'You must not look,' he said: but now I believe
Without seeing, what harm can it be to gaze?
He said, 'It is a secret.' Oh but in love
There are no secrets! and how can I ever prove
My love till I know what it is I might betray?

So ran the fatal argument; and so,
Closer than night, equivocal as a spy,
Into bed between them stole the lie . . .
She rose and lit her lamp. In the hall below
The harp strings broke, the wine jars all ran dry.

Heavy with sight, alarmed at new-born shadows,
She groped towards him. Night drew back in awe,
And the light became a clear, impassable window
Through which her love could gaze but never go.
The lamp burned brighter, inflamed by what it saw.

O moon-white brow and milky way of flesh!
Wings like a butterfly's on a warm stone

Trembling asleep! O rod and fount of passion,
Godlike in act, estranged in revelation! —
Once you were mine, were me, for me alone.

O naked light upon our marriage bed,
Let me touch you again and be consumed!
No reaching through the radiance you shed?
Breaking my faith, myself I have betrayed.
We that were one are two. Thus am I doomed.

She grasped her knife, but it refused the breast
She offered. Trying a finger on his arrows
She pricked herself, and love was dispossessed
By love of love, which means self-love. Unblest,
Unchecked — what a serpent flame letched at her
        marrow!

Darkness she craved now — but oblivion's pall
Not the true night of union. Anyway
The lamp would not blow out. Along the wall
A taloned shadow-beast began to crawl
Fawning and glum toward its naked prey.

A drop of burning oil upon his bare
Shoulder awoke him. Shuddering he beheld
Crusted over that face so innocent-fair,
The hangdog look, the dissolute anxious glare
Of lust, and knew his treasure had been spoiled.

So he passed from her, and at last she learnt
How blind she had been, how blank the world can be
When self-love breaks into that dark room meant
For love alone, and on the innocent
Their nakedness dawns, outraging mystery.

Followed the tasks — millet seed, poppy seed
And all. They keep her fingers busy, bind
A gaping heart. She tells the grain like beads:

Yet it is not her penance, it is her need
Moves mercy, proves and touches the Divine.

Dear souls, be told by me. I would not take
Love as a gift, and so I had to learn
In the cold school of absence, memory's ache,
The busy, barren world of mend and make,
That my god's love is given but never earned.

Baucis and Philemon

You see those trees on the hillside over the lake
Standing together — a lime tree and an oak —
With a stone circle around them? A strange thing
To find two trees wearing a marriage ring,
You say? You would not, if you knew their story. Yes,
They are wedded: the roots embrace, the leaves caress
One another still. You can hear them gossip together,
Murmuring commonplaces about the weather,
Rocked by gusts of memory, like the old.
In this evening light their wall is a hoop of gold . . .

Philemon gazed into the cooling hearth,
And the hearth stared listlessly back at one whose fire
Was all but ash. His hands hung down like dry leaves
Motionless in a summer's aftermath —
Planter's hands, they could make anything grow.
So labourers sit at the end of a day or a lifetime.
The old man drowsed by the fire, feeling his death
Ripen within him, feeling his lifetime gone
Like a may-fly's day, and nothing to show for all
The works and days of his hands but a beaten path
Leading nowhere and soon to be overgrown.
Beside him, Baucis absently traced her memories

Which seemed a brood of children scattered long since
Among far lands; but always in him, her own —
Husband and child — where they began, they ended.
Knuckled like bark, palmed thin as a saint's relics,
Her hands rested from love. There was love in the shine
Of the copper pans, the thrift of a mended coverlet,
The scrubbed and sabbath face of the elm-wood table.
But now this wordless love, which could divine
Even in sleep his qualms and cares, awoke
And out of the speaking silence between them, heard

    To dwindle down, to gutter and go out,
Consenting to the dark or jerking agonized
Shadows on the white faces round me!
The year goes out in a flash of chrysanthemum:
But we, who cell by cell and
Pang upon pang are dragged to execution,
Live out the full dishonour of the clay.
A bright bewildered April, a trance-eyed summer —
Mirage of immortality: then
The mildew mists, the numbing frosts, and we
Are rotting on the bough, who ripen to no end
But a maggot's appetite.
Where are my memories? Who has taken the memories
I stored against these winter nights, to keep me warm?
My past is under snow — seed-beds, bud-grafts,
Flowering blood, globed hours, all shrouded, erased:
There I lie, buried alive before my own eyes.
Are we not poor enough already
That the gods must take away? —

                    'Hush, my dear,'
Said Baucis, and laid her finger upon his lips
Like a holy wafer. 'We must not even dream
Ill of the gods. I too fear Death, but I fear
Him most because he will take one of us first
And leave the other alive. I fear his cruelty
Less than his charity.'

There was a knock at the door.
Her heart cried out — He has come for us both, bless him!
But it was only a couple of tramps or tinkers,
A bearded one and a younger, begging food,
All other doors in the village closed against them.
'You are welcome. It's nice to have company once in a
      while,'
She said to the grimy wayfarers, and strewed
Clean coverlets on the willow-wood couch for them
To rest while she blew up the fire again. Philemon
Brought out a well-smoked ham and his autumn fruit —
Radishes, endives, apples and plums, a honeycomb.
'You wandering folk see much of the world,' he said.
'Ah yes, there's nothing my father has not seen
In his time,' the young man answered: 'except perhaps
An eagle nesting with two turtle doves.'
The other smiled in his beard: his gaze, serene
As if it could weigh the gods and find them wanting,
Weighed now those hands like skeleton leaves, the
      bird-boned
Pair and the crumbs they shared, a copper pan
Gleaming, a rickety table freshened with mint.
All was amenity there, a calm sunshine
Of the heart. The young stranger, whose grey eyes
Were full of mischief and messages, winked at the elder:
'They could not treat us handsomer if we were gods.'
His companion nodded — at once the windless trees
In the orchard danced a fandango — and raised his cup
Of beechwood, charged to the brim with home-made wine:
'Philemon, a toast! I give you — your memories.'
He drained the cup; and when he had put it down,
It was still brimming. And in Philemon's soul
Welled up a miraculous spring, the wished release.

    I am blind no longer. My joys have come home to me
Dancing in gipsy colours from oblivion.
Back on their boughs are the fruits of all my seasons
Rosy from sleep still, ripened to the core.

Look at the autumn trees content with their workaday
Russet and the grass rejoicing for mere greenness,
As the spring paths I trod through garden, through orchard,
Were content with violets. Oh chime and charm
Of remembered Junes, of killer frosts returning
To smile and be forgiven! Oh temperate haze
Maturing my yesterdays, promise of good morrows! —
Seventy years have I lived with Contentment,
And now for the first time I see her face.
Now I can thank the gods, who mercifully
Changed my despair into a cup full of blessings
And made a vision grow where a doubt was planted.

Baucis, weeping and smiling, knelt to adore
The elder god: who said, 'You had a wish too?'
With a glance at her husband's shadowless face, she replied,
'You have done one miracle. How could I ask more?
He is content. What more did I ever ask?'
'Nevertheless, an unspoken prayer shall be answered
When the prayer is good, and not to have voiced the prayer
Is better. Death shall not part you. Now follow me.'
They helped each other up the slow hillside
Like pilgrims, while the two gods went before.
When they looked back, their cottage in the combe below
Was changed — cob walls to pearl and thatch to gold —
A lodge for deity, almost as marvellous
As the wonder in their eyes. 'Ah, that is no
Miracle,' Hermes said, 'or if it is,
The miracle is yours.' Then Zeus affirmed, 'The seed
Hears not the harvest anthem. I only show you
A jewel your clay has formed, the immortal face
Of the good works and days of your own hands:
A shrine after my heart. Because I know you
Faithful in love to serve my hearth, my earth,
You shall stay here together when you go . . . '

They climbed that hill each evening of their lives
Until, one day, their clasped hands uttered leaves

And the tired feet were taken underground.
'Goodbye, dear wife,' he called as the bark closed round,
And his branches upheld the cry in a carol of birds.
She yearned to his oaken heart, with her last words
Sweet as lime blossom whispering on the air —
'It's not goodbye.'
　　　　　　　　We found them growing there
And built the wall about them; not that they need
A ring to show their love, or ever did.

Ariadne on Naxos

(A Dramatic Monologue)

Between the hero's going and the god's coming
She paced a flinty shore, her windflower feet
Shredded and bleeding, but the flesh was numb
Or the mind too delirious to heed
Its whimpers. From the shore she vainly dredged
The deep horizon with a streaming eye,
And her strained ears like seashells only fetched
A pure pale blare of distance. Listlessly
She turned inland. Berries on bushes there
Watched her like feral eyes: she was alone:
The darkening thicket seemed a monster's fur,
And thorn trees writhed into a threat of horns.
She walks a knife-edge here, between the woe
Of what is gone and what will never go.

O many-mooded One, you with the bared
Horizons in your eye, death in your womb,
Who draw the mariner down to a choked bed
And write his name upon an empty tomb —
Strangle him! Flay the flesh from his dishonoured
Bones, and kiss out his eyes with limpets! — No,

Drown my words! Who is the faithless now? Those eyes
Were true, my love. Last night, beside the myrtle,
You said 'For ever', and I saw the stars
Over your head, and then the stars were lost in
The flare and deluge of my body's dawn.
False dawn. I awoke. Still dark. Your print upon me
Warm still. A wind, chilling my nakedness,
Lisped with the sound of oars. It was too dark
To see the wake of your bold, scuttling ship,
Or I'd have reeled you back on that white line,
As once . . . Is it because I saved you then
That you run from me as from a place accursed?

What is it in the bushes frightens me so?
A hide for nothing human. Coalfire eyes
Penning me on the beach. You had a kingdom
In your eyes. When you looked at me with love,
Were you only seeing a way to it through me?
I am a girl, unversed in the logic of heroes —
But why bring me so far, rescuing me
From my father's rage, to leave me on this island
For the wild beasts? leave me like a forgotten
Parcel, or a piece of litter you had no time
To bury when you had used it under the myrtle?
Already a star shows. It is a day, an age
Since we came here. Oh, solitude's the place
Where time congeals and memories run wild.

I put the ball of thread into your hands.
It is my own heartstrings I am paying out
As you go down the tunnel. I live with you
Through the whole echoing labyrinth, and die
At each blind corner. Now you have come back with
A bloody sword, a conqueror's tired smile.
For you, the accustomed victory: for me,
Exultation, miracle, consummation.
Embracing you, the steel between us, I took
That blood upon myself, sealing our bond
Irrevocably with a smear of blood,
Forgetting that a curse lifted falls elsewhere

And weighs the heavier, forgetting whose blood it was.
Did you hear my mother's willing, harsh outcry
Under the bull, last night? and shrink from your
Accomplice in the hot act, remembering
Whose daughter she is and whose unnatural son
She helped you butcher in the labyrinth?

   I was a royal child, delicately nurtured,
Not to be told what happened once a year
Beneath the mosaic floor, while the court musicians
Played louder and my father's face went still
As a bird listening for worms. But the maids gossiped;
And one day, when I was older, he explained —
Something about war crimes, lawful deterrents,
Just compensation for a proved atrocity.
It seemed nothing to do with flesh and blood,
The way he talked. Men have this knack for embalming
And burying outraged flesh in sleek abstractions.
Have you, too, found already a form of words
To legitimize the murdering of our love?
Ah well, I was not guiltless — never a thought for
The writhing give-and-take of those reparations
Until, with the last consignment of living meat
To be fed to the man-bull in the maze, you came.

   You with the lion look among that huddle
Of shivering whelps — I watched you from the gate-tower
And trembled, not in pity, but afraid
For my own world's foundations. When our hands
Touched at the State Reception, I knew myself
A traitor, wishing that world away, and found
My woman's heart — sly, timorous, dangerous creature,
Docile but to the regent of her blood,
Despising the complexities men build
To cage or to hush up the brute within.
What were parents and kingdom then? or that
Poor muzzled freak in the labyrinth, my brother?
— Forgotten all. Forgetfulness, they say,
Is the gods' timeliest blessing or heaviest curse.
A bundle of fear and shame, too much remembering,

I lie, alone, upon this haunted isle.
   A victim for a victim is the law.
Is there no champion strong enough to break
That iron succession? Listen! What is this word
The bushes are whispering to the offshore breeze?
'Forget'? No. Tell me again. 'Forgive.' A soft word.
I'll try it on my tongue. Forgive. Forgive . . .
How strangely it lightens a bedevilled heart!
Come out of the thorn thicket, you, my brother,
My brother's ghost! Forgive the clue, the sword!
Forgive my fear of you! Dead, piteous monster,
You did not will the hungry maze, the horns,
The slaughter of the innocents. Come, lay
Your muzzle on my forsaken breast, and let us
Comfort each other. There shall be no more blood,
No more blood. Our lonely isle expands
Into a legend where all can dream away
Their crimes and wounds, all victims learn from us
How to redeem the Will that made them so.

   So on the dark shore, between death and birth,
Clasping a ghost for comfort, the girl slept.
Gently the night breeze bore across that firth
Her last, relinquishing sob: like tears unwept,
Windflowers trembled in the eye of night
Under the myrtle. Absence whirred no more
Within her dreamless head, no victim cried
Revenge, no brute fawned on its conqueror.
At dawn, far off, another promise broken,
The hero's black sail brought his father death.
But on that island a pale girl, awoken
By more than sunlight, drew her quick, first breath
Of immortality, seeing the god bend down
And offer a hoop of stars, her bridal crown.

Seasonable Thoughts
for Intellectuals

(at Portland Bill, 1949)

Cold chisels of wind, ice-age-edged,
Hammered hard at the marble block of
This mutilated island. Wind like a wedge
Splitting the cross-grained, bitter sea.
What a pity no artist or master mason
Aims the blows blind Nature lays on!

Flint flakes of a wintry sea
Shaling off the horizon
In endless, anonymous, regimental order.
Fish or fowl should laugh to see
Such penitential hordes of water.
Not so merrily laugh we.

A shag, wave-hopping in emblematic flight
Across that molten iron, seems
Less a bird than the shadow of some bird above,
So invulnerably it skims.
But there's no sun, and Neptune's unreflective,
And anyway, who wants a fowl's directive? . . .

O sea, with your wolverine running,
Your slavering over the land's end,
Great waves gulping in granite pot-holes,
Smacking your lips at the rocks you'd devour,
Belching and belly-rumbling in caves,
Sucking your teeth on the shingle! —
How sad to think that, before
You've more than nibbled a trillionth of the meal,

A piece of jelly which came from your maw
Many aeons ago, and contracted a soul,
May atomize earth and himself and you —
Yes, blow the whole bloody issue back into the blue.

The Pest

That was his youthful enemy, fouling the azure
With absolute mirk risen from god knows where —
A zero mood, action's and thought's erasure,
Impassable as rock, vapid as air.
When angels came, this imbecile thing infesting
His home retired to its sanctum below stairs;
But emerged, sooner or later, clammily testing
His hold on grace, his bond with the absent stars:
Till the horror became a need, the blacked-out sky
A promise that his angels would reappear,
A proof of light. Then the curse played its sly
Last trick — it thinned away, it was never there.
If it has gone for good, will he mope and die
Like a pauper with the lice washed out of his hair?

Almost Human

The man you know, assured and kind,
Wearing fame like an old tweed suit —
You would not think he has an incurable
Sickness upon his mind.

Finely that tongue, for the listening people,
Articulates love, enlivens clay;
While under his valued skin there crawls
An outlaw and a cripple.

Unenviable the renown he bears
When all's awry within? But a soul
Divinely sick may be immunized
From the scourge of common cares.

A woman weeps, a friend's betrayed,
Civilization plays with fire —
His grief or guilt is easily purged
In a rush of words to the head.

The newly dead, and their waxwork faces
With the look of things that could never have lived,
He'll use to prime his cold, strange heart
And prompt the immortal phrases.

Before you condemn this eminent freak
As an outrage upon mankind,
Reflect: something there is in him
That must for ever seek

To share the condition it glorifies,
To shed the skin that keeps it apart,
To bury its grace in a human bed —
And it walks on knives, on knives.

Love and Pity

Love without pity is a child's hand reaching,
A behemoth trampling, a naked bulb within   *Huge creature*
A room of delicate tones, a clown outraging
The heart beneath the ravished, ravisher skin.
Pity without love is the dry soul retching,
The strained, weak azure of a dog-day sky,
The rescuer plunging through some thick-mined region
Who cannot rescue and is not to die.
Pitiless love will mean a death of love —
An innocent act, almost a mercy-killing:
But loveless pity makes a ghost of love,
Petrifies with remorse each vein of feeling.
Love can breed pity. Pity, when love's gone,
Bleeds endlessly to no end — blood from stone.

The Tourists

Arriving was their passion.
Into the new place out of the blue
Flying, sailing, driving —
How well these veteran tourists knew
Each fashion of arriving.

Leaving a place behind them,
There was no sense of loss: they fed
Upon the act of leaving —
So hot their hearts for the land ahead —
As a kind of pre-conceiving.

Arrival has stern laws, though,
Condemning men to lose their eyes

If they have treated travel
As a brief necessary disease,
A pause before arrival.

And merciless the fate is
Of him who leaves nothing behind,
No hostage, no reversion:
He travels on, not only blind
But a stateless person.

Fleeing from love and hate,
Pursuing change, consumed by motion,
Such arrivistes, unseeing,
Forfeit through endless self-evasion
The estate of simple being.

Final Instructions

For sacrifice, there are certain principles —
Few, but essential.

I do not mean your ritual. This you have learnt —
The garland, the salt, a correct use of the knife,
And what to do with the blood:
Though it is worth reminding you that no two
Sacrifices ever turn out alike —
Not where this god is concerned.

The celebrant's approach may be summed up
In three words — patience, joy,
Disinterestedness. Remember, you do not sacrifice
For your own glory or peace of mind:
You are there to assist the clients and please the god.

It goes without saying
That only the best is good enough for the god.
But the best — I must emphasize it — even your best
Will by no means always be found acceptable.
Do not be discouraged:
Some lizard or passing cat may taste your sacrifice
And bless the god: it will not be entirely wasted.

But the crucial point is this:
You are called only to *make* the sacrifice:
Whether or no he enters into it
Is the god's affair; and whatever the handbooks say,
You can neither command his presence nor explain it —
All you can do is to make it possible.
If the sacrifice catches fire of its own accord
On the altar, well and good. But do not
Flatter yourself that discipline and devotion
Have wrought the miracle: they have only allowed it.

So luck is all I can wish you, or need wish you.
And every time you prepare to lay yourself
On the altar and offer again what you have to offer,
Remember, my son,
Those words — patience, joy, disinterestedness.

The House Where
I Was Born

An elegant, shabby, white-washed house
With a slate roof. Two rows
Of tall sash windows. Below the porch, at the foot of
The steps, my father, posed
In his pony trap and round clerical hat.
This is all the photograph shows.

No one is left alive to tell me
In which of those rooms I was born,
Or what my mother could see, looking out one April
Morning, her agony done,
Or if there were pigeons to answer my cooings
From that tree to the left of the lawn.

Elegant house, how well you speak
For the one who fathered me there,
With your sanguine face, your moody provincial charm,
And that Anglo-Irish air
Of living beyond one's means to keep up   Keeping up a front.
An era beyond repair.

Reticent house in the far Queen's County,
How much you leave unsaid.
Not a ghost of a hint appears at your placid windows
That she, so youthfully wed,
Who bore me, would move elsewhere very soon
And in four years be dead.

I know that we left you before my seedling
Memory could root and twine
Within you. Perhaps that is why so often I gaze

At your picture, and try to divine
Through it the buried treasure, the lost life —
Reclaim what was yours, and mine.

I put up the curtains for them again
And light a fire in their grate:
I bring the young father and mother to lean above me,
Ignorant, loving, complete:
I ask the questions I never could ask them
Until it was too late.

'The Years O'

The days are drawing in,
A casual leaf falls.
They sag — the heroic walls;
Bloomless the wrinkled skin
Your firm delusions filled.
What once was all to build
Now you shall underpin.

The day has fewer hours,
The hours have less to show
For what you toil at now
Than when long life was yours
To cut and come again,
To ride on a loose rein —
A youth's unbroken years.

Far back, through wastes of ennui
The child you were plods on,
Hero and simpleton
Of his own timeless story,
Yet sure that somewhere beyond
Mirage and shifting sand
A real self must be.

Is it a second childhood,
No wiser than the first,
That we so rage and thirst
For some unchangeable good?
Should not a wise man laugh
At desires that are only proof
Of slackening flesh and blood?

Faster though time will race
As the blood runs more slow,
Another force we know:
Fiercer through narrowing days
Leaps the impetuous jet,
And tossing a dancer's head
Taller it grows in grace.

Time to Go

The day they had to go
Was brilliant after rain. Persimmons glowed
In the garden behind the castle.
Upon its wall lizards immutably basked
Like vitrified remains
Of an archaic, molten summer. Bronze
Cherubs shook down the chestnuts
From trees over a jetty, where fishing nets
Were sunshine hung out in skeins
To dry, and the fishing boats in their little harbour
Lay breathing asleep. Far
And free, the sun was writing, rewriting ceaselessly
Hieroglyphs on the lake —
Copying a million, million times one sacred
Vanishing word, peace.
The globed hours bloomed. It was grape-harvest season,

And time to go. They turned and hurried away
With never a look behind,
As if they were sure perfection could only stay
Perfect now in the mind,
And a backward glance would tarnish or quite devalue
That innocent, golden scene.
Though their hearts shrank, as if not till now they knew
It was paradise where they had been,
They broke from the circle of bliss, the sunlit haven.
Was it for guilt they fled?
From enchantment? Or was it simply that they were driven
By the migrant's punctual need?
All these, but more — the demand felicity makes
For release from its own charmed sphere,
To be carried into the world of flaws and heartaches,
Reborn, though mortally, there.

So, then, they went, cherishing their brief vision.
One watcher smiled to see
Them go, and sheathed a flaming sword, his mission
A pure formality.

Dedham Vale, Easter 1954

For E.J.H.

It was much the same, no doubt,
When nature first laid down
These forms in his youthful heart.
Only the windmill is gone
Which made a miller's son
Attentive to the clouds.

This is the vale he knew —
Its games of sun and shower,

Willow and breeze, the truant
Here-and-there of the Stour;
And an immutable church tower
To polarize the view.

Yet, earnestly though we look
At such hard facts, the mill,
The lucid tower and the lock
Are something less than real.
For this was never the vale
He saw and showed unique —

A landscape of the heart,
Of passion nursed on calm,
Where cloud and stream drew out
His moods, and love became
A brush in his hand, and the elm tree
Lived like a stroke of art.

His sunburst inspiration
Made earthly forms so true
To life, so new to vision,
That now the actual view
Seems a mere phantom, through
Whose blur we glimpse creation.

It wears a golden fleece
Of light. However dull
The day, one only sees here
His fresh and flying colours —
A paradise vale where all is
Movement and all at peace.

The Great Magicians

To fish for pearls in Lethe,
Wash gold from age-long grief;
To give infinity a frame,
The may-fly a reprieve:

In a calm phrase to utter
The wild and wandering sky;
To reconcile a lover's Eden
With a madman's sty:

To mediate between
The candle and the moth;
To plug time's dripping wound, or spin
A web across hell's mouth:

Such feats the great magicians
Found within their powers,
Whose quick illusions bodied out
A world more whole than ours.

But the hollow in the breast
Where a God should be —
This is the fault they may not
Absolve nor remedy.

From Moods of Love

5

Inert, blanched, naked, at the gale's last gasp
Out of their drowning bliss flung high and dry
Above the undertow, the breakers' rasp,
With shells and weed and shining wrack they lie.
Or, as an isle asleep with its reflection
Upon the absolute calm, each answers each
In the twin trance of an unflawed affection
That shows the substance clear, the dream in reach.
By one arched, hollowing, toppling wave uptossed
Together on the gentle dunes, they know
A world more lucid for lust's afterglow,
Where, fondly separate, blind passion fused
To a reflective glass, each holds in trust
The other's peace, and finds his real self so.

7

Shells, weed, discoloured wrack — a spring tide's litter
Dully recalling its lost element,
And one you live with, quarrelsome or complying,
Are all that's left of Aphrodite's birth.
Gone is the power she gave you to delight her,
The period of grace, so quickly spent,
When the day's walk was a white dream of flying,
Earth a far cry, she a sufficient earth.

Whether long use has now choked your desire
With its own clinker, or, abruptly parted
At love's high noon, incredulous you have stood
Suffering her absence like a loss of blood
Week after week, still, by the god deserted,
You worship relics of a sacred fire.

9

If love means exploration — the divine
Growth of a new discoverer first conceived
In flesh, only the stranger can be loved:
Familiar loving grooves its own decline.

If change alone is true — the ever-shifting
Base of each real or illusive show,
Inconstancy's a law: the you that now
Loves her, to otherness is blindly drifting.

But chance and fretting time and your love change her
Subtly from year to year, from known to new:
So she will always be the elusive stranger,
If you can hold her present self in view.

Find here, in constant change, faithful perceiving,
The paradox and mode of all true loving.

Last Words

Suppose, they asked,
You are on your death-bed (this is just the game
For a man of words),
With what definitive sentence will you sum
And end your being? . . . Last words: but which of me
Shall utter them?

— The child, who in London's infinite, intimate darkness
Out of time's reach,

Heard nightly an engine whistle, remote and pure
As a call from the edge
Of nothing, and soon in the music of departure
Had perfect pitch?

— The romantic youth
For whom horizons were the daily round,
Near things unbiddable and inane as dreams,
Till he had learned
Through his hoodwinked orbit of clay what Eldorados
Lie close to hand?

— Or the ageing man, seeing his lifelong travel
And toil scaled down
To a flimsy web
Stranded on two dark boughs, dissolving soon,
And only the vanishing dew makes visible now
Its haunted span?

Let this man say,
Blest be the dew that graced my homespun web.
Let this youth say,
Prairies bow to the treadmill: do not weep.
Let this child say,
I hear the night bird, I can go to sleep.

From The Gate (1962)

To Peggy and Jeremy

The Gate

For Trekkie

In the foreground, clots of cream-white flowers (meadow-
    sweet?
Guelder? Cow parsley?): a patch of green: then a gate
Dividing the green from a brown field; and beyond,
By steps of mustard and sainfoin-pink, the distance
Climbs right-handed away
Up to an olive hilltop and the sky.

The gate it is, dead-centre, ghost-amethyst-hued,
Fastens the whole together like a brooch.
It is all arranged, all there, for the gate's sake
Or for what may come through the gate. But those white
    flowers,
Craning their necks, putting their heads together,
Like a crowd that holds itself back from surging forward,
Have their own point of balance — poised, it seems,
On the airy brink of whatever it is they await.

And I, gazing over their heads from outside the picture,
Question what we are waiting for: not summer —
Summer is here in charlock, grass and sainfoin.
A human event? — but there's no path to the gate,
Nor does it look as if it was meant to open.
The ghost of one who often came this way
When there was a path? I do not know. But I think,
If I could go deep into the heart of the picture

From the flowers' point of view, all I would ask is
Not that the gate should open, but that it should
Stay there, holding the coloured folds together.
We expect nothing (the flowers might add), we only
Await: this pure awaiting —
It is the kind of worship we are taught.

View From An Upper Window

For Kenneth and Jane Clark

From where I am sitting, my windowframe
Offers a slate roof, four chimneypots,
One aerial, half of a leafless tree,
And sky the colour of dejection. I could
Move my chair; but, London being
What it is, all would look much the same
Except that I'd have the whole of that tree.
Well, window, what am I meant to do
With the prospect you force me to dwell upon — this
     tame
And far from original *aperçu*?

I might take the picture for what it can say
Of immediate relevance — its planes and tones,
Though uninspiring, significant because
Like history they happened to happen that way.
Aerial, chimneypots, tree, sky, roof
Outline a general truth about towns
And living together. It should be enough,
In a fluctuating universe, to see they are there
And, short of an atom bomb, likely to stay.
But who wants truth in such everyday wear?

Shall I, then, amplify the picture? track
The roof to its quarry, the tree to its roots,
The smoke just dawdling from that chimneystack
To the carboniferous age? Shall I lift those slates
And disclose a man dying, a woman agape
With love? Shall I protract my old tree heavenwards,

Or set these aerial antennae to grope
For music inaudible, unborn yet? But why,
If one's chasing the paradigm right forward and back,
Stop at embryo, roots, or sky?

Perhaps I should think about the need for frames.
At least they can lend us a certain ability
For seeing a fragment as a kind of whole
Without spilling over into imbecility.
Each of them, though limited its choice, reclaims
Some terra firma from the chaos. Who knows? —
Each of *us* may be set here, simply to compose
From a few grains of universe a finite view,
By One who occasionally needs such frames
To look at his boundless creation through?

The Newborn

(D.M.B.: April 29th, 1957)

This mannikin who just now
Broke prison and stepped free
Into his own identity —
Hand, foot and brow
A finished work, a breathing miniature —
Was still, one night ago,
A hope, a dread, a mere shape we
Had lived with, only sure
Something would grow
Out of its coiled nine-month nonentity.

Heaved hither on quickening throes,
Tossed up on earth today,
He sprawls limp as a castaway
And nothing knows
Beside the warm sleep of his origin.

Soon lips and hands shall grope
To try the world; this speck of clay
And spirit shall begin
To feed on hope,
To learn how truth blows cold and loves betray.

Now like a blank sheet
His lineaments appear;
But there's invisible writing here
Which the day's heat
Will show: legends older than language, glum
Histories of the tribe,
Directives from his near and dear —
Charms, curses, rules of thumb —
He will transcribe
In his own blood to write upon an heir.

This morsel of man I've held —
What potency it has,
Though strengthless still and naked as
A nut unshelled!
Every newborn seems a reviving seed
Or metaphor of the divine,
Charged with the huge, weak power of grass
To split rock. How we need
Any least sign
That our stone age can break, our winter pass!

Welcome to earth, my child!
Joybells of blossom swing,
Lambs and lovers have their fling,
The streets run wild
With April airs and rumours of the sun.
We time-worn folk renew
Ourselves at your enchanted spring,
As though mankind's begun
Again in you.
This is your birthday and our thanksgiving.

Circus Lion

Lumbering haunches, pussyfoot tread, a pride of
Lions under the arcs
Walk in, leap up, sit pedestalled there and glum
As a row of Dickensian clerks.

Their eyes are slag. Only a muscle flickering,
A bored, theatrical roar
Witness now to the furnaces that drove them
Exultant along the spoor.

In preyward, elastic leap they are sent through paper
Hoops at another's will
And a whip's crack: afterwards, in their cages,
They tear the provided kill.

Caught young, can this public animal ever dream of
Stars, distances and thunders?
Does he twitch in sleep for ticks, dried water-holes,
Rogue elephants, or hunters?

Sawdust, not burning desert, is the ground
Of his to-fro, to-fro pacing,
Barred with the zebra shadows that imply
Sun's free wheel, man's coercing.

See this abdicated beast, once king
Of them all, nibble his claws:
Not anger enough left — no, nor despair —
To break his teeth on the bars.

232

Getting Warm —
Getting Cold

For Tamasin

We hid it behind the yellow cushion.
'There's a present for you,' we called,
'Come in and look for it.' So she prowled
About the suddenly mysterious room —
'Getting warm,' she heard, 'getting cold.'

She moved in a dream of discovery, searching
Table and shelf and floor —
As if to prolong the dream, everywhere
But behind that cushion. Her invisible present
Was what she lived in there.

Would she never find it? Willing her on,
We cried, 'you're cold, you're warm,
You're burning hot,' and the little room
Was enlarged to a whole Ali Baba's cave
By her eyes' responsive flame.

May she keep this sense of the hidden thing,
The somewhere joy that enthralled her,
When she's uncountable presents older —
Small room left for marvels, and none to say
'You are warmer, now you are colder.'

Walking Away

For Sean

It is eighteen years ago, almost to the day —
A sunny day with the leaves just turning,
The touch-lines new-ruled — since I watched you play
Your first game of football, then, like a satellite
Wrenched from its orbit, go drifting away

Behind a scatter of boys. I can see
You walking away from me towards the school
With the pathos of a half-fledged thing set free
Into a wilderness, the gait of one
Who finds no path where the path should be.

That hesitant figure, eddying away
Like a winged seed loosened from its parent stem,
Has something I never quite grasp to convey
About nature's give-and-take — the small, the scorching
Ordeals which fire one's irresolute clay.

I have had worse partings, but none that so
Gnaws at my mind still. Perhaps it is roughly
Saying what God alone could perfectly show —
How selfhood begins with a walking away,
And love is proved in the letting go.

This·Young Girl

This young girl, whose secret life
Vagues her eyes to the reflective, lucent
Look of the sky topping a distant
Down beyond which, invisible, lies the sea —

What does she mark, to remember, of the close things
That pearl-calm gaze now shines upon? . . .
Her mother, opening a parasol,
Drifts over the hailed-with-daisies lawn:

Head full of designs, her father
Is pinned to a drawing board: two brothers settle
For cool jazz in the barn: a little
Sister decides to become Queen Pocahontas.

Or is it the skyline viewed from her attic window
Intimating the sea, the sea
Which far off waits? or the water garden
Fluent with leaves and rivulets near by,

That will be her memory's leitmotif?
All seems acceptable — an old house sweetened
By wood-ash, a whole family seasoned
In dear pursuits and country gentleness.

But her eyes elude, this summer's day. Far, far
Ahead or deep within they peer,
Beyond those customary things
Towards some Golden Age, that is now, is here.

An Upland Field

By a windrowed field she made me stop.
'I love it — finding you one of these,'
She said; and I watched her tenderly stoop
Towards a sprig of shy heartsease
Among the ruined crop.

'Oh but look, it is everywhere!'
Stubble and flint and sodden tresses
Of hay were a prospect of despair:
But a myriad infant heartsease faces
Pensively eyed us there.

Long enough had I found that flower
Little more common than what it is named for —
A chance-come solace amid earth's sour
Failures, a minute joy that bloomed for
Its brief, precocious hour.

No marvel that she, who gives me peace
Wherein my shortening days redouble
Their yield, could magically produce
From all that harshness of flint and stubble
Whole acres of heartsease.

Not Proven

(a Dramatic Monologue)

for George Rylands

NOTE:Madeleine Hamilton Smith was tried for murder, at Edinburgh, in 1857. She died in the United States of America, aged 92, in 1928.

So. I am dying. Let the douce young medico
Syrup his verdict, I am not deceived.
You pity me, boy? a shrunk old woman dying
Alone in an alien country? Sir, you have chosen
The wrong woman to pity. There was a girl
Seventy-two years ago — high-coloured, handsome,
The belle of the Glasgow ballrooms — gave herself
Body and soul to a wheedling mannikin,
And went down into hell through him. Pity
Her, if pity you must — though she asked none
Except from her dwarf-souled lover — not this crumpled
Dead-letter of flesh, yellow as the press-cuttings
I keep in my workbox there. You wonder why
I treasure such things? I was a heroine,
A nine-days' marvel to an admiring world.
No, sir, my wits are not astray. Those cuttings —
They're my citations for valour. Close, come closer.
The panel's voice grows weak. You are very young.
Tell me, what does it mean to you — the name of
Madeleine Smith? . . .

                              Now he is gone at last,
The nice wee doctor, leaving a prescription
And an unuttered question in the room —
A question I have seen for seventy years
In every eye that knew me, and imagined
In every eye that would not rest on mine.
They got no sign from me — those speiring eyes:
Long ago I learnt to outface even
My own, soliciting me from the cold mirror,

237

As I outfaced them all in court for nine days —
Beetle-eyes of journalists crawling busily
Over me; jurymen's moth-eyes fluttering at mine
And falling, scorched; bat-eyes darting around me.
And after the trial, a drift of letters offering
Marriage, or fornication. Chivalrous
Young fools, wishful to comfort a wronged innocent;
Used-up philanderers dreaming of new sensations
In bed with a murderess; they too were drawn
To the mystery behind this brow, the sphinx.
  My secret! Ah, the years have mossed it over,
The lettering on the stone's illegible now.
    HERE LIE THE REMAINS OF MADELEINE,
    DAUGHTER OF JAMES SMITH, WIDOW OF GEORGE
    WARDLE, IN HOPE OF EVERLASTING OBLIVION.
    SHE WAS TRIED FOR THE MURDER OF HER
    LOVER, PIERRE EMILE L'ANGELIER, BY THE
    ADMINISTRATION OF ARSENIC. THE VERDICT
    OF THE COURT: NOT PROVEN.
    THE REST WAS SILENCE.

                                  Beneath that slab I have lain
Seventy years — the remains of a gallant girl
Whom passion, flaring up too high, too sudden,
Blackened like a lamp-chimney. Oh, long-dead flame!
They say there comes a lightening before death.
Light, any light, come — ray of mercy or bale-fire —
And run some stitch of meaning through my life,
The shreds and snippets of that Madeleine,
Her after-life!

                        Well, there were compensations,
They think? The wicked prospered? George was kind,
Smooring the question in his heart. Affluence
We had: travel: the house in Onslow Gardens:
Artists and thinkers round us — William Morris,
William de Morgan: the Social Democrat Club.
Yes, I was quite a firebrand for those days . . .
  A brand plucked from the burning: charred, chastened —
So you would figure me, all you respectable
Fathers and mothers of nubile daughters who

Must cool their blood with albums, prayers, tea-parties?
I hear your judgment, hypocrites, mealy-mouthed
Over the porridge at the mahogany sideboards:
'Guilty or innocent of murder, she
Has shamed our womanhood. Illicit love
Were shame enough; but that a female should
Write to her lover, exulting in the act,
Baring herself in words to acknowledge pleasure —
Depraved! Unnatural! Doubtless she repents now.'
Repentance? Shame? Little you know, Papa,
Nor you, Lord Justice-Clerk, sitting in judgment
On me, where lies the core of my remorse,
The cancer of my shame . . .

                No, they are dead,
Those stuffed men — long ago dead. Foolish Madeleine,
Dreaming yourself once more back to the trial,
The aftermath! Aye, at one bound, as if
The years between were a wee burn to jump
And not the insipid mere, the bottomless pit
Which has swallowed up my youth, my pride, my graces
Like dumped rubbish, and still been unfulfilled.
Would I return, live it again, to keep death
Waiting a while for me? Would the old actress
Re-live her greatest triumph! — and not to stay death;
To spurn him from the pinnacle of her fame.
Yes, I would walk as then, flushed with achievement,
Out of the cheering courtroom through the chill
Silence of Rowaleyn (Papa frock-coated,
A plaster figure of repudiation,
The family Jehovah buttoned up in
Self-righteous outrage; brothers and sisters cowed
Less by his wrath than by my flung defiance:
Mother, of course, had taken to her bed) —
Stride like a tragic heroine, through that last
Ordeal, into my life's long anti-climax.

      Dusk already? What time is it? My skin
Sweats cold. Doctor! You cannot let me die —
Not yet! Madeleine Smith must go to court:

Her trial is not yet over. She must live
Through the command performance once again.
Doctor! . . . Doctor, are you familiar with
The signs of poisoning by arsenic? No,
He is not here. Contempt of court. And I
Despise it too — the cant and rigmarole
Of the Law. Quick then, Madeleine, dress yourself:
Demure black mantle, and the straw scoop-bonnet
Trimmed with white ribbon, leaving your face naked
To all the prurient, cringing eyes — unveiled,
But in its cold, bold calm inviolable.
Madeleine takes the dock — how did they put it? —
With the air of a belle entering a ballroom.

                               See,
The room fills up with shadows — a sibilant audience
Of ghosts: they rise: Hope, Handyside and Ivory,
Robed and bewigged, come soberly on — dead men
To sit in judgment on a dying actress.
No, no, my Lords, it is not you, tricked out
In gravity and fine feathers, who will make
This play immortal; nor you, Lord Advocate,
Plaiting your rope of logic round my neck;
Nor even you, John Inglis, Dean of Faculty,
My eloquent defender: no, it is I,
The silent heroine of the wordy drama,
Who pack your theatre day after day.
Let them drone on — what do I care? — over
That trash, that reptile thing which died writhing.
      Ah, how the drab years fly up like a blind
At *his* vile touch, to show the lighted past!
And through that scene, a play behind a play,
Moncrieff, Lord Advocate, frigidly weaving
His figured plot . . . On such and such occasions
The panel purchased arsenic, stating that
It was to kill rats, or for her complexion.
On such and such occasions the deceased
Took ill; and the third time he died of it.
We've no eye-witness: but no doubt the panel

Administered the poison in a cup
Of cocoa which she handed to her lover
That last night through the basement window of
The house in Blythswood Square, the scene of previous
Assignations — passed it across the space
Between her window and the railings, where
She had been used to put her letters for
Pierre Emile L'Angelier to pick up —
Those passionate letters which he threatened now
To show her father, if she would not abandon
Her purpose of wedding another, William Minnoch.
To all the panel's desperate entreaties
That he should return her letters, L'Angelier
Was adamant. Rather than be exposed
As a vicious wanton and ruined irretrievably,
She murdered him. That is the Crown's case.
　　　'What did you think, Miss Smith, of the Lord
　　　　Advocate's
Address?' *When I have heard the Dean of Faculty,*
I'll tell you. I never like to give an opinion
Until I have heard both sides of the question.
By God! I was a pert young lassie then,
And fearless too — letting my wit dance
On the scaffold's trap-door, over the drop, the quick-lime —
So you believed? Or a monster from the Pit,
Murderess, whore, with the vibrant, mordant tongue
Of the damned? But I was neither, I tell you; only
A woman, the husk that's left of a woman after
Premature birth, when her rich, quickened body
Has dropped a stillborn thing (dropped? aborted?)
A love, conceived in ecstasy, that became
A deadweight burden, a malignant growth
Of self-disgust . . .
　　　　　　　　　But listen, the Dean of Faculty
Rises to address the jury. Listen.
Gentlemen of the Jury, the charge against the prisoner
is murder, and the punishment of murder is death;
and that simple statement is sufficient to suggest to us

the awful solemnity of the occasion
which brings you and me face to face.
Inglis! Listen to me, Inglis. You must drive home
The point about my letters. The prosecution
Has said I would go any length to stop
Those letters being revealed. And so I would have,
Almost, but not to the folly of — oh, they must
Realize there was no surer way of having
My letters to him made public than for Emile
To die by poison. Do they suppose that I
Would not see this? They insult my intelligence. But
The panel is a woman: all men know
The weaker sex have little power of reason.
Weaker? Pah! Why, why must I be silent
While self-important lawyers play at ball
With my life? No, I *will* speak!

                        My Lords, and you
Gentlemen of the jury, listen to me.
Lay by your masks, all this majestic flummery —
You, lords of creation, who keep us women
To fawn on you, be petted, brought to heel —
And think: although nature has trained our bodies
To fawn, our hearts to love subjection, how would
A woman — slave and Spartacus to her sex —
Once she'd revolted from this rule of nature,
Loathe him for whom nature had made her kneel!
And what if such a woman found her master,
Not weak, vain, tyrannous merely — you are all so —
But abject, sirs, abject as a maggot
That clings to the flesh it has gorged on? a maggot who,
After his first meal, sermonized to me
About the weakness of *my* flesh! Ach, men,
The moral hypochondriacs, for ever
Coddling their timid minds against the real,
Medicining themselves with patent lies
And sedative abstractions — look, how bravely
Cowardice makes a conscience for them all!
I am accused of poisoning my lover.

Bring *him* to trial, I say. Let Pierre Emile
L'Angelier be arraigned for poisoning love.
Aye, the deep wells of my awakened body,
The pent abundance, and the dancing fountains
That leapt and wept for him like paradise trees
In diamond leaf — he tainted them. How soon
My springs went bitter and the loving cup
Tasted metallic! . . . Sirs, you have marvelled at
My strange composure. Do you not recognize
The calm of a face prepared for burial? Which,
Which is the tragic victim? — one who dies
Vomiting up a trumpery soul? or one
Who, legend-high in love, proud as Diana,
Awakes to find her matchless Prince deformed
Into a Beast, a puny, whimpering lapdog?
Oh waste, waste, waste! Sirs, I plead guilty of
Self-mutilation. Cutting that hateful image
Out of my heart, I should have bled to death:
But hatred's a fine cautery for such wounds,
And love as wild as mine needs but a flick of
Indignity or disrelish to become
That searing, healing, all-redeeming hatred.
But what do you know of such things, my Lords,
With your tame wives and farthing-dips of lust?
As for this trial of yours — a man has ceased,
A paltry creature whom my passion exalted
Into a figment of its own white fire.
That furnace proved him dross. He is better dead,
My Lords . . .
      My Lords! Hear me out! Why do they —
Hope, Handyside and Ivory — why withdraw,
Dissolve to moonshine? Moonshine, and a haze of
Branches knitted above me. I am caged in
From the star-daisied heaven. Ah, my rowans:
The garden of Rowaleyn, and beside me —
Emile! Emile, wake up! I have had a terrible
Dream. I dreamt that I had — dreamt that you
Were dead. Comfort me. Do not be cold.

You are not angry with me? I am your wife now,
Truly your wife, the woman you've created
As God created woman. I worship you.
Listen to my heart, Emile — close, come closer —
How the blood pulses for you, calm and crazing
As torrents of moonshine; crazed and calmed by you.
Husband, speak to me. Do not be afraid:
They are all asleep in the house. Papa is sleeping
The sleep of the self-righteous: he'll never dream
That I'd creep out to you, your cat, your vixen,
For a midsummer mating. Are you ashamed
Because I am so shameless in love? But I
Have high blood in these veins, dare-devil blood:
My kin's not all the halfway kind who live
Haltered by prudence and propriety — no,
Remember, I am Madeleine *Hamilton* Smith.
Why are you silent, Emile? — and so cold,
Clay-cold to my fevered lips! The night is chill
For June, and you are delicate: you must go, love:
Your Mimi must not be the death of you.
Go quickly, then. We shall soon be together —
One bed, one life — for always. I will coax
Papa, or else defy him. I am all yours now.
Quick! — by the side gate . . . Why will you not go?
Are you frozen to my side? Leave me! No, no more
Loving — get away from me! You shall not —

>   *Oh!*

The fearful dream! Loathing. A clay man:
Incubus from the grave. What was he doing
Here at my bedside? trying to fright me into
Death-bed confession? Always he misprized me,
Misjudged: it is not well to underrate
A woman such as I . . . Had I been born
Fifty years later, I should leave the world
Richer for me and be remembered as
A maker, a pioneer, not an enigma.
What an end for the Lucifer who rebelled
Against their sanctimonious, whiskered god —

To be smuggled out, like a prisoner who has served
Life-sentence, by a side door of the jail,
Fameless and futureless!
                              Who's this at my door
In black among the shadows? A minister?
I have nothing to say to you. Nothing. He draws
Nearer. It is the minister of bone.
Sir, I shall be no burden for you to carry.
I am light and small now — small in your arms:
A wisp of flesh; some courage; and what weighs
Heavier than they — my secret. I can trust you
With it. Hold me up. It is hard to speak,
To breathe. Whose hand — the cup of poison? His?
Mine? But so long ago it happened, how
Can I be sure? Their busy arguments
Hummed in my ears like echoes from a dream,
Making unreal all that had passed between us,
Emile and me, till I became two phantasms —
One innocent, one guilty, and the truth
Went down in the gulf between them, the real I —
What she had done or not done — sinking away
From me, dubious, hidden, lost, amid
A fog and welter of words.
                              It lies too deep now
In the black ooze. My heart quakes. The sea-bed
Heaves. Last agony. Heaves to give up its dead.
I cannot. Sir, have mercy on me. Make haste.
I am heavy with you. Deliver me.
Madeleine, Madeleine, tell me the truth.
I have forgotten . . . long ago . . . forgotten.

Ideal Home

1

Never would there be lives enough for all
The comely places —
Glimpsed from a car, a train, or loitered past —
That lift their faces
To be admired, murmuring 'Live with me.'

House with a well,
Or a ghost; by a stream; on a hill; in a hollow: breathing
Woodsmoke appeal,
Fresh paint, or simply a prayer to be kept warm,
Each casts her spell.

Life, claims each, will look different from my windows,
Your furniture be
Transformed in these rooms, your chaos sorted out here.
Ask for the key.
Walk in, and take me. Then you shall live again.

2

. . . Nor lives enough
For all the fair ones, dark ones, chestnut-haired ones
Promising love —
I'll be your roof, your hearth, your paradise orchard
And treasure-trove.

With puritan scents — rosemary, thyme, verbena,
With midnight musk,
Or the plaintive, memoried sweetness tobacco-plants
Exhale at dusk,
They lure the footloose traveller to dream of

One fixed demesne,
The stay-at-home to look for his true self elsewhere.
I will remain
Your real, your ideal property. Possess me.
Be born again.

3

If only there could be lives enough, you're wishing? . . .
For one or two
Of all the possible loves a dozen lifetimes
Would hardly do:
Oak learns to be oak through a rooted discipline.

Such desirableness
Of place or person is chiefly a glamour cast by
Your unsuccess
In growing your self. Rebirth needs more than a change of
Flesh or address.

Switch love, move house — you will soon be back where
　　　you started,
On the same ground,
With a replica of the old romantic phantom
That will confound
Your need for roots with a craving to be unrooted.

Fisherman and/or Fish

There was a time when I,
The river's least adept,
Eagerly leapt, leapt
To the barbed, flirtatious fly.

Thrills all along the line,
A tail thrashing — the sport
Enthralled: but which was caught,
Which reeled the other in?

Anglers aver they angle
For love of the fish they play
(Arched spine and glazing eye,
A gasping on the shingle).

I've risen from safe pools
And gulped hook line and sinker
(Oh, the soft merciless fingers
Fumbling at my gills!)

Let last time be the last time
For me with net or gaff.
I've had more than enough
Of this too thrilling pastime.

The river's veteran, I
Shall flick my rod, my fin,
Where nothing can drag me in
Nor land me high and dry.

The Antique Heroes

Faultlessly those antique heroes
    Went through their tests and paces,
Meeting the most extraordinary phenomena
    With quite impassive faces.

Dragons, chimeras, sirens, ogres
    Were all in the day's work;
From acorn to dryad, from home to the Hesperides
    No further than next week.

There was always someone who would give them
    something
    Still more impossible to do,
And a divinity on call to help them
    See the assignment through.

The functions of the heroine were,
    Though pleasurable, more narrow —
Receiving a god, generally Zeus,
    And breeding another hero.

It gave life an added interest for all
    Compliant girls, to know
That a bull, a swan, a yokel might be
    Deity incognito.

Scholars dispute if such tales were chiefly
    The animist's childwise vision,
Ancestor-snobbery, or a kind of
    Archaic science-fiction.

Well, I have seen a clutch of hydras
    Slithering round W.C.2,
And Odysseus striding to the airport. I think
    Those tales could be strictly true.

'Said the Old Codger'

When Willie Yeats was in his prime,
Said the old codger,
Heroic frenzy fired his verse:
He scorned a poet who did not write
As if he kept a sword upstairs.

Nowadays what do we find,
Said the old codger,
In every bardlet's upper room?
— Ash in the grate, a chill-proof vest,
And a metronome.

The Unexploded Bomb

Two householders (semi-detached) once found,
Digging their gardens, a bomb underground —
Half in one's land, half in t'other's, with the fence between.
Neighbours they were, but for years had been
Hardly on speaking terms. Now X. unbends
To pass a remark across the creosoted fence:
'Look what I've got! . . . Oh, you've got it too.
Then what, may I ask, are you proposing to do
About this object of yours which menaces my wife,
My kiddies, my property, my whole way of life?'
'Your way of life,' says Y., 'is no credit to humanity.
I don't wish to quarrel; but, since you began it, I
Find your wife stuck-up, your children repel me,
And let me remind you that we too have the telly.
This bomb of mine —'
                          'I don't like your tone!
And I must point out that, since I own

More bomb than you, to create any tension
Between us won't pay you.'
                              'What a strange misapprehension!'
Says the other: 'my portion of bomb is near
Six inches longer than yours. So there!'

'They seem,' the bomb muttered in its clenched and
        narrow
Sleep, 'to take me for a vegetable marrow.'

'It would give me,' said X., 'the very greatest pleasure
To come across the fence now with my tape-measure —'
'Oh no,' Y. answered, 'I'm not having you
Trampling my flowerbeds and peering through
My windows.'
                        'Oho,' snarled X., 'if that's
Your attitude, I warn you to keep your brats
In future from trespassing upon my land,
Or they'll bitterly regret it.'
                              'You misunderstand.
My family has no desire to step on
Your soil; and my bomb is a peace-lover's weapon.'

Called a passing angel, 'If you two shout
And fly into tantrums and keep dancing about,
The thing will go off. It is surely permissible
To say that your bomb, though highly fissible,
Is in another sense one and indivisible;
By which I mean — if you'll forgive the phrase,
Gentlemen — the bloody thing works both ways.
So let me put forward a dispassionate proposal:
Both of you, ring for a bomb-disposal
Unit, and ask them to remove post-haste
The cause of your dispute.'

                        X. and Y. stared aghast
At the angel. 'Remove my bomb?' they sang
In unison both: 'allow a gang

To invade my garden and pull up the fence
Upon which my whole way of life depends?
Only a sentimental idealist
Could moot it. I, thank God, am a realist.'

The angel fled. The bomb turned over
In its sleep and mumbled, 'I shall soon discover,
If X. and Y. are too daft to unfuse me,
How the Devil intends to use me.'

Requiem for the Living

REQUIEM

Grant us untroubled rest. Our sleep is fretted,
Anxious we wake, in our terrestrial room.
What wastes the flesh, what ticks below the floor will
Abort all futures, desecrate the tomb.

Let healing grace now light upon us. All flesh
Lives with its death. But may some shaft unblind
Soon our sick eyes, lest the death we choose to live with
And then must die be the murder of mankind.

Peace in our time: else upon earth a timeless
Pause of unbeing, sterile, numb and null —
Spiritus mundi, a smudge of breath wiped off
Glass; earth revolving, an idiot skull.

O living light, break through our shroud! Release
Man's mind, and let the living sleep in peace.

KYRIE ELEISON

Because we are hypnotized by a demon our will has

conjured: because we play for safety with dangerous
power, and dare not revoke: because we injure the
tissue of creation —

> Have pity upon us.

Whether in the pursuit of knowledge, the name of
freedom, or the course of duty, I serve humanity's
programme for suicide; or whether inert I
acquiesce —

> Have pity upon me.

I am the young who have no time in trust, no time
for belief; the old who reserve the sacrament of
violence: I am what struts or chaffers on a
crumbling edge of existence —

> Have pity upon me.

In the hour of our death, and in the day of our
judgment —

> Have pity upon us.

DIES IRAE

Day of wrath, oh ruthless day
When humankind shall melt away:
Day of wrath when in a flash
History shall burn to ash.

Turning keys upon the dials
Shall unloose the furious phials;
Then the trumpeting blasts be heard —
Art, law, science, all absurd.

From a lucid heaven foresee
Monstrous that epiphany
Of man's calculated error
Break in light and brood in terror:

Skin flayed off the skeleton,
Ghosts of men burnt into stone,
Uberant rivers boiling dry,
Cities sucked up into the sky.

All too late then for repenting
Of the powers we are mis-spending.
We could only pray that doom
Fall sheer on us and fast consume;

Pray the loud heat-stroke spare us not
For the soundless rain to rot
Our angry blood, corrupt our bone —
Remnants of life that crawl and moan;

Spare us not to see this earth
Travail with a second birth,
Monsters multiply and breed
From a joyless, tainted seed.

Look how the sun of nature dips
Toward evil's dark apocalypse!
How near the ages' growth is blighted,
Man in his brilliancy benighted!

Day of wrath, oh ruthless day
When humankind shall melt away:
Day of wrath when in a flash
Past and future turn to ash.

*   *   *

BENEDICTUS

Blessed are they who come
At need, in mercy's name
To walk beside the lame,
Articulate for the dumb.

Blessed who range ahead
Of man's laborious trek,
Survey marsh, desert, peak,
Signal a way to tread.

Blessed whose faith defies
The mighty, welds the weak;
Whose dreaming hopes awake
And ring like prophecies.

Blessed who shall release
At this eleventh hour
Us thralls of evil power
And lift us into peace.

* * *

RESPONSORIUM

Free us from fear, we cry. Our sleep is fretted,
Anxious we wake, in our terrestrial room.
What wastes the flesh, what ticks below the floor would
Abort all futures, desecrate the tomb.

Free us from fear. The shapes that loom around us
Darkening judgment, freezing all that's dear
Into a pose of departure — these are shadows
Born of man's will and bodied by his fear.

May the white magic of the child's wayfaring,
Wonderful earth — our present from the dead,
And the long vistas of mankind slow maturing
Lighten the heart and clear the feverish head!

O living light, break through our shroud! Release
Man's mind, and let the living sleep in peace!

255

From The Room and Other Poems
(1965)

To Elizabeth Bowen

On Not Saying Everything

This tree outside my window here,
Naked, umbrageous, fresh or sere,
Has neither chance nor will to be
Anything but a linden tree,
Even if its branches grew to span
The continent; for nature's plan
Insists that infinite extension
Shall create no new dimension.
From the first snuggling of the seed
In earth, a branchy form's decreed.

Unwritten poems loom as if
They'd cover the whole of earthly life.
But each one, growing, learns to trim its
Impulse and meaning to the limits
Roughed out by me, then modified
In its own truth's expanding light.
A poem, settling to its form,
Finds there's no jailer, but a norm
Of conduct, and a fitting sphere
Which stops it wandering everywhere.

As for you, my love, it's harder,
Though neither prisoner nor warder,
Not to desire you both: for love
Illudes us we can lightly move
Into a new dimension, where
The bounds of being disappear
And we make one impassioned cell.
So wanting to be all in all
Each for each, a man and woman
Defy the limits of what's human.

Your glancing eye, your animal tongue,
Your hands that flew to mine and clung
Like birds on bough, with innocence
Masking those young experiments
Of flesh, persuaded me that nature
Formed us each other's god and creature.
Play out then, as it should be played,
The sweet illusion that has made
An eldorado of your hair
And our love an everywhere.

But when we cease to play explorers
And become settlers, clear before us
Lies the next need — to re-define
The boundary between yours and mine;
Else, one stays prisoner, one goes free.
Each to his own identity
Grown back, shall prove our love's expression
Purer for this limitation.
Love's essence, like a poem's, shall spring
From the not saying everything.

Derelict

For A.D. Peters

The soil, flinty at best, grew sour. Its yield
Receding left the old farm high and dry
On a ledge of the hills. Disused, the rutted field-
Track fades, like the sound of footsteps, into a sigh
For any feet to approach this padlocked door.
The walls are stained and cracked, the roof's all rafter.
We have come where silence opens to devour
Owl-cry, wind-cry, all human memories . . . After
So many working life-times a farm settles

For leisure, and in the tenth of a life-time goes
To seed . . . A harrow rusts among harsh nettles.
She who in love or protest grew that rose
Beneath her window, left nothing else behind
But a mangle in the wash-house. The rose now
Looks mostly thorn and sucker; the window's blind
With cobwebs. Dilapidated! — even the low
Front wall is ragged: neighbours have filched its stone
To build their pigsties, maybe; but what neighbours? —
Never did a farm stand more alone.
Was it the loneliness, then, and not their labour's
Poor yield that drove them out? A farmer's used
To the silence of things growing, weather breeding.
More solitude, more acres. He'd be amused
To hear it's human company he was needing,
With a wife to bake, wash, mend, to nag or share
The after-supper silence, children to swing
From those rheumatic apple trees; and where
The docks run wild, his chained-up mongrel barking
If anyone climbed a mile off on the hill.
He'd not abandon cheerfully a place
In which he'd sunk his capital of skill
And sweat. But if earth dies on you, it's no disgrace
To pull up roots . . . Now, all that was the farm's —
The same demands of seasons, the plain grit
And homely triumph — deepens and informs
The silence you can hear. Reverence it.

St. Anthony's Shirt

'We are like the relict garments of a Saint: the same and not the same: for
the careful Monks patch it and patch it: till there's not a thread of the
original garment left, and still they show it for St Anthony's shirt.'
Keats: Letter to Reynolds

This moving house of mine —how could I care
If, wasting and renewing cell by cell,
It's the ninth house I now have tenanted?

I cannot see what keeps it in repair
Nor charge the workmen who, its changes tell,
Build and demolish it over my head.

Ninth house and first, the same yet not the same —
Are there, beneath new brickwork, altering style,
Viewless foundations steady through the years?
Hardly could I distinguish what I am
But for the talkative sight-seers who file
Through me, the window-view that clouds or clears.

The acting, speaking, lusting, suffering I
Must be a function of this house, or else
Its master principle. Is I a sole
Tenant created, recreated by
What he inhabits, or a force which tells
The incoherent fabric it is whole?

If master, where's the master-thread runs through
This patchwork, piecemeal self? If occupant
Merely, the puppet of a quarrelsome clique,
How comes the sense of selfhood as a clue
Embodying yet transcending gene and gland?
The I, though multiple, is still unique.

I walk these many rooms, wishing to trace
My frayed identity. In each, a ghost
Looks up and claims me for his long-lost brother —
Each unfamiliar, though he wears my face.
A draught of memory whispers I was most
Purely myself when I became another:

Tending a sick child, groping my way into
A woman's heart, lost in a poem, a cause,
I touched the marrow of my being, unbared
Through self-oblivion. Nothing remains so true
As the outgoingness. This moving house
Is home, and my home, only when it's shared.

Fishguard to Rosslare

From all my childhood voyages back to Ireland
Only two things remembered: gulls afloat
Off Fishguard quay, littering a patch of radiance
Shed by the midnight boat.

And at dawn a low, dun coast shaping to meet me,
An oyster sky opening above Rosslare . . .
I rub the sleep from my eyes. Gulls pace the moving
Mast-head. We're almost there.

Gulls white as a dream on the pitch of Fishguard harbour,
Paper cut-outs, birds on a lacquered screen;
The low coastline and the pearl sky of Ireland;
A long sleep in between.

A sleep between two waking dreams — the haven,
The landfall — is how it appears now. The child's eye,
Unpuzzled, saw plain facts: I catch a glint from
The darkness they're haunted by.

Seven Steps in Love

'I dreamed love was an angel,
But her finger-tip is laid
Like the peine forte et dure upon
My breast, and I'm afraid.

'I am afraid, afraid.
The letter-box rattles a threat,
Disaster seeps through my window-frame,
Takes me by the throat.'

Sure, earth changes colour
And the heart's oppressed —
It's the storm of rebirth you fear — when *she*
Points a man at your breast.

Oh she's the wheedling goddess
With a strap behind her back:
She'll hand you a bunch of roses
And lay you on the rack;

Stretch you upon your lover's absence,
Wring you dry of tears,
Brainwash you into believing
You're dead till he climbs the stairs.

And if at last for each other
Body and mind you strip,
She'll pin her undated farewell note
Onto the pillow-slip.

Give in, give in, fond lovers,
And she'll starve you with wanting more:
Refrain, refrain, and she crams you
With yeasty dreams to the craw.

She has no heart for mercy,
Treats honour as a clown:
But when her naked eye selects you,
Better lie down, lie down.

2

Where autumn and high midsummer meet, there's a touch
Of desperation — rose-beds ready to flare
Their last, holidays nearly over, a premonition
Of bonfire and frost in the air.

Veterans of the game, they watched the agents
Of that great power, disguised as usual
In quite transparent innocence, dawdle across the frontier
Disarming and casual

As tourists. A main force deployed from both.
Silently the soft perimeters fell.
Then key positions, yielding at a collusive whisper,
Betrayed the citadel.

Each occupied by the other now, they exchange
Rations, arms, campaign-talk: nothing matters
But more and more to surrender. See the vanquished
    crown with
Olive those sweet invaders.

The everyday opens into a paradise garden.
Gold roses spring through pavements, and a spray
Of freesia freshens the dusty room. For a while, winter
Seems two life-times away.

When eyes go dark and bodies
Nakedly press home,
Let all else be dumb,
Louder sing the sensual glee,
Louder the nerves thrum.

Stand off, you cowled observer
Who eye love's act askance.
Shameless of tongue, of hands,
Body shall make the awkward soul
Jump to its commands.

Only the wry soul answers
In ridicule or disgust.
Praise, man, that flurry of dust —
Your rutting animal: moon-gold woman,
Be candid of your lust.

Now the respectful lover,
Fleshed upon his prey
Brute hunger to allay,
Is one with roughneck ancestors
Millenniums away.

Now she is the tumid
Ocean he rides and reaps:
Wave upon wave she leaps
Against him; then her dissolute power
Gulps him down, and sleeps.

When eyes go dark and bodies
One to another fly,
Let not the soul decry
What wisdom's born from dialogues
Of wanton breast and thigh.

* * *

The Romantics

Those two walked up a chancel of beech trees
Columnar grey, and overhead there fluttered
Fan-vaultings of green leaf. She moved with chastity's
Dancing step, he dull with love unuttered.
She is all Artemis, he thought, and I
Her leashed and clownish hound. But he miscalled her
Who dreamily saw at the ride's far end an O of sky
Like love-in-a-mist, herself pure white, an altar.

The vows exchanged, their love pronounced eternal,
They learn how altar stands for sacrifice.
All changes — beechwood chancel into a cramped tunnel;
Huntress to victim; hound, throwing off disguise,
To faithless hero. Soon he'll take the knife and start
To carve his way out of her loving heart.

Stephanotis

Pouring an essence of stephanotis
Into his bath till the panelled, carpeted room
Breathed like a paradise fit for sweltering houris,
He lapsed through scent and steam

To another bathroom, shires and years away —
A makeshift one tacked on to
The end of a cottage, it smelt of rusting pipes,
Damp plaster. In that lean-to

One night she sprinkled the stephanotis
He'd given her — a few drops of delicate living
Tasted by two still young enough to need
No luxury but their loving.

They are long parted, and their essence gone.
Yet even now he can smell,
Infused with the paradise scent, that breath of rusty
Water and sweating wall.

Pietà

Naked, he sags across her cumbered knees,
Heavy and beautiful like the child she once
Aroused from sleep, to fall asleep on the next breath.

The passion is done,
But death has not yet stiffened him against her,
Nor chilled the stripling grace into a dogma.
For a timeless hour, imagined out of marble,
He comes back to his mother, he is all
And only hers.

And it is she whom death has magnified
To bear the burden of his flesh — the arms
Excruciated no more, the gash wiped clean.
A divine, dazed compassion calms her features.
She holds all earth's dead sons upon her lap.

Elegy for a Woman Unknown

(F.P.)

1

At her charmed height of summer —
Prospects, children rosy,
In the heart's changeful music
Discords near resolved —
Her own flesh turned upon her:
The gross feeder slowly
Settled to consume her.

Pain speaks, bearing witness
Of rank cells that spawn
To bring their temple down.
Against such inmost treachery
Futile our protesting:
The body creates its own
Justice and unjustness.

Three times flesh was lopped,
As trees to make a firebreak.
(In their natural flowering
Beautiful the trees.)
Three times her enemy leapt
The gap. Three years of dying
Before the heart stopped.

Upon the shrinking islands
Of flesh and hope, among
Bitter waves that plunged,
Withdrew to lunge yet deeper,

Patient, unreconciled,
She wrote poems and flung them
To the approaching silence.

Upon the stretching hours
Crucified alone,
She grew white as a stone
Image of endurance;
Soft only to the cares
Of loved ones — all concern
For lives that would soon lack hers.

Dying, did she pass through
Despair to the absolute
Self-possession — the lightness
Of knowing a world indifferent
To all we suffer and do,
Shedding the clung-to load
Of habit, illusion, duty?

You who watched, phase by phase,
Her going whose life was meshed
With yours in grief and passion,
Remember now the unspoken,
Unyielding word she says —
How, in ruinous flesh,
Heroic the heart can blaze.

2

Island of stone and silence. A rough ridge
Chastens the innocent azure. Lizards hang
Like their own shadows crucified on stone
(But the heart palpitates, the ruins itch
With memories amid the sunburnt grass). Here sang
Apollo's choir, the sea their unloosed zone.
Island of stillness and white stone.

Marble and stone — the ground-plan is suggested
By low walls, plinths, lopped columns of stoa, streets
Clotted with flowers dead in June, where stood
The holy place. At dusk they are invested
With Apollonian calm and a ghost of his zenith heats.
But now there are no temples and no god:
Vacantly stone and marble brood,

And silence — not the silence after music,
But the silence of no more music. A breeze twitches
The grass like a whisper of snakes; and swallows there are,
Cicadas, frogs in the cistern. But elusive
Their chorusing — thin threads of utterance, vanishing stitches
Upon the gape of silence, whose deep core
Is the stone lions' soundless roar.

Lions of Delos, roaring in abstract rage
Below the god's hill, near his lake of swans!
Tense haunches, rooted paws set in defiance
Of time and all intruders, each grave image
Was sentinel and countersign of deity once.
Now they have nothing to keep but the pure silence.
Crude as a schoolchild's sketch of lions

They hold a rhythmic truth, a streamlined pose.
Weathered by sea-winds into beasts of the sea,
Fluent from far, unflawed; but the jaws are toothless,
Granulated by time the skin, seen close,
And limbs disjointed. Nevertheless, what majesty
Their bearing shows — how well they bear these ruthless
Erosions of their primitive truth!

Thyme and salt on my tongue, I commune with
Those archetypes of patience, and with them praise
What in each frantic age can most incline
To reverence; accept from them perfection's myth —
One who warms, clarifies, inspires, and flays.
Sweetness he gives but also, being divine,
Dry bitterness of salt and thyme.

The setting sun has turned Apollo's hill
To darker honey. Boulders and burnt grass.
A lyre-thin wind. A landscape monochrome.
Birds, lizards, lion shapes are all stone-still.
Ruins and mysteries in the favouring dusk amass,
While I reach out through silence and through stone
To her whose sun has set, the unknown.

* * *

For Rex Warner
On His Sixtieth Birthday

'The hawk-faced man' — thirty-five years ago
I called him — 'who could praise an apple
In terms of peach and win the argument' . . .
Oxford between the wars. I at the age of dissent
From received ideas, admiring a man so able
At undermining the crusted status quo.

But he was no sophist, this unsophisticated
Son of a Modernist clergyman, who came down
From a Cotswold height with the larks of Amberley
And the lays of Catullus running wild in his head. We,
Two green youths, met by chance in a Jacobean
Quad. From that term our friendship's dated.

Friendship, I'd guess, has not much more to do
With like minds, shared needs, than with rent or profit:
Nor is it the love which burns to be absolute, then dies
By inches of ill-stitched wounds, of compromise:
But a kind of grace — take it or leave it.
'Keeping up' a friendship means it is through.

That grace I accept. When he returns at last
From Egypt, Greece, the States, we take up where
We left. Right friendships are that homing, each to the other,
On frequencies unchanged through time or weather.
And still, though bulkier, he'll appear
In focus with the young self I knew first. —

Scholar, wing three-quarter, and bird-watcher:
Self-contained, yet an affable bar-crony:
A mind of Attic dash and clarity,
Homeric simpleness, and natural charity
For all but intellectual cliques and their baloney. —
So was he then. And since, each new departure

Proved him, though wayward, all of a piece.
Working a spell of allegoric art,
In *The Wild Goose Chase* and *The Aerodrome*
He formed a style intrinsic, dry and firm —
Revetment against the chaos in his and a nation's heart —
As, centuries ago, Thucydides.

Fable or fact, living and dead, he carries
Greece near his heart. Rocks, olives, temples, sea and sun
In lucid paradigm express
His tonic scepticism, cordial address.
Pericles and Prometheus spoke through one
Loved by Sikelianós and great Seferis.

Enough that in a pretentious age, when all —
Love, politics, art, right down to money — is cheapened,
He'll take each issue for what it's worth, not wincing,
Inflating, prancing his ego there, romancing
A tragic fall: if deaths have happened
In him, through him, he never preached at the funeral.

It's friendship we return to in the end:
Past selves are kept alive in it, a living

Communion flows from their dead languages. A home
Enlarged by absences, mellowed by custom,
Undemanding, simply taking and giving,
Is he, our sixty-year-old friend.

My Mother's Sister

I see her against the pearl sky of Dublin
Before the turn of the century, a young woman
With all those brothers and sisters, green eyes, hair
She could sit on; for high life, a meandering sermon

(Church of Ireland) each Sunday, window-shopping
In Dawson Street, picnics at Killiney and Howth . . .
To know so little about the growing of one
Who was angel and maid-of-all-work to my growth!

— Who, her sister dying, took on the four-year
Child, and the chance that now she would never make
A child of her own; who, mothering me, flowered in
The clover-soft authority of the meek.

Who, exiled, gossiping home chat from abroad
In roundhand letters to a drift of relations —
Squires', Goldsmiths, Overends, Williams' — sang the songs
Of Zion in a strange land. Hers the patience

Of one who made no claims, but simply loved
Because that was her nature, and loving so
Asked no more than to be repaid in kind.
If she was not a saint, I do not know

What saints are . . . Buying penny toys at Christmas
(The most a small purse could afford) to send her
Nephews and nieces, she'd never have thought the shop
Could shine for me one day in Bethlehem splendour.

Exiled again after ten years, my father
Remarrying, she faced the bitter test
Of charity — to abdicate in love's name
From love's contentful duties. A distressed

Gentle woman housekeeping for strangers;
Later, companion to a droll recluse
Clergyman brother in rough-pastured Wexford,
She lived for all she was worth — to be of use.

She bottled plums, she visited parishioners.
A plain habit of innocence, a faith
Mildly forbearing, made her one of those
Who, we were promised, shall inherit the earth.

. . . Now, sunk in one small room of a Rathmines
Old people's home, helpless, beyond speech
Or movement, yearly deeper she declines
To imbecility — my last link with childhood.

The battery's almost done: yet if I press
The button hard — some private joke in boyhood
I teased her with — there comes upon her face
A glowing of the old, enchanted smile.

So, still alive, she rots. A heart of granite
Would melt at this unmeaning sequel. Lord,
How can this be justified, how can it
Be justified?

This Loafer

In a sun-crazed orchard
Busy with blossomings
This loafer, unaware of
What toil or weather brings,
Lumpish sleeps — a chrysalis
Waiting, no doubt, for wings.

And when he does get active,
It's not for business — no
Bee-lines to thyme or heather,
No earnest to-and-fro
Of thrushes: pure caprice tells him
Where and how to go.

All he can ever do
Is to be entrancing,
So that a child may think,
Upon a chalk-blue chancing,
'Today was special. I met
A piece of the sky dancing.'

Terns

Sunlit over the shore
Terns — a flock of them — flew,
With swordplay supple as light
Criss-crossing the charmed blue.
They seemed one bird, not a score —
One bird of ubiquitous flight,
One blade so swift in the fence
It flickers like twenty men's,
Letting no thought of a scar,
No fatal doubt pierce through.

Oh whirl and glide, the cut
And thrust of the dazzling terns,
Weaving from joy or need
Such quick, momentous patterns!
If we shall have opted out
Of nature, may she breed
Something more tern-like, less
Inept for togetherness
Than we, who have lost the art
Of dancing to her best tunes.

Apollonian Figure

Careful of his poetic p's and q's,
This self-possessed master of circumspection
Enjoyed a *marriage blanc* with the Muse,
Who never caught his verse in an erection.

Some praise the lapidary figure: but
With due respect to the attendant's spiel,
That fig-leaf there, so elegantly cut —
Just what, if anything, does it conceal?

A Relativist

He raged at critic, moralist — all
That gang who with almightiest gall
Lay claim to the decisive vote
In separating sheep from goat.

So on the last day, when he's got
His breath back again, it will not
Be goats or sheep that rouse his dudgeon
But the absurdity of judging.

From The Whispering Roots
and some Later Poems

For Sean and Anna

Avoca, Co. Wicklow

Step down from the bridge.
A spit of grass points
At the confluence.

Tree he sat beneath
Spoiled for souvenirs,
Looks numb as driftwood.

A pretty fellow
In stone broods over
The meeting waters.

His words came alive
But to music's flow,
Like weeds in water.

I recall my aunt, my second mother,
Singing Tom Moore at the old rectory
Harmonium — *The Last Rose of Summer,*
She is far from the Land — her contralto
Scoop, the breathy organ, an oil lamp lit.
Words and tune met, flowed together in one
Melodious river. I drift calmly
Between its banks. Sweet vale of Avoca,
She is still young, I a child, and our two
Hearts like thy waters are mingled in peace.

Dublin tradesman's son,
Byron's friend, the pet
Of Whig drawing-rooms.

Feted everywhere,
Everywhere at home,
He sang of exile

And death, tailoring
Country airs to a
Modish elegance.

Let the waters jig
In a light glitter,
So the source run full.

Near Ballyconneely, Co. Galway

1

A stony stretch. Grey boulders
Half-buried in furze and heather,
Purple and gold — Connemara's
Old bones dressed in colours
Out of a royal past.

Inshore the sea is marbled
And veined with foam. The Twelve Pins
Like thunderclouds hewn from rock
Or gods in a cloudy fable
Loom through an overcast.

The roofless dwellings have grown
Back to the earth they were raised from,
And tune with those primordial
Outcrops of grey stone
Among the furze and the heather.

Where man is dispossessed
Silence fills up his place
Fast as a racing tide.
Little survives of our West
But stone and the moody weather.

2

Taciturn rocks, the whisht of the Atlantic
The sea-thrift mute above a corpse-white strand
Pray silence for those vanished generations
Who toiled on a hard sea, a harsher land.

Not all the bards harping on ancient wrong
Were half as eloquent as the silence here
Which amplifies the ghostly lamentations
And draws a hundred-year-old footfall near.

Preyed on by gombeen men, expropriated
By absentee landlords, driven overseas
Or to mass-burial pits in the great famines,
They left a waste which tourists may call peace.

The living plod to Mass, or gather seaweed
For pigmy fields hacked out from heath and furze —
No eye to spare for the charmed tourist's view,
No ear to heed the plaint of ancestors.

Winds have rubbed salt into the ruinous homes
Where turf-fires glowed once: waves and seagulls keen
Those mortal wounds. The landscape's an heroic
Skeleton time's beaked agents have picked clean.

Ass in Retirement

Ass
orbits
a firm stake:
each circle round
the last one is stamped
slow and unmomentous
like a tree-trunk's annual rings.

He does not fancy himself as a tragedian,
a circumference mystic or a treadmill hero,
nor takes he pride in his grey humility.
He is just one more Irish ass
eating his way round the clock,
keeping pace with his own appetite.

Put out to grass, given a yard more rope
each week, he takes time off from what's under his nose
only to bray at rain-clouds over the distant bog;
relishes asinine freedom — having to bear
no topple of hay, nor cleeves crammed with turf;
ignorant that he'll come in time

to the longest tether's end,
then strangle or accept
that stake. Either way
on the endless
grass one day
he'll drop
dead.

At Old Head, Co. Mayo

In a fisherman's hat and a macintosh
He potters along the hotel drive;
Croagh Patrick is far beyond him now the locust
Has stripped his years of green.
Midges like clouds of memory nag
The drooped head. Fish are rising
Under his hat. He stops against the view.

All is a brushwork vision, a wash
Of new-laid colour. They come alive —
Fuchsia, grass, rock. The mist, which had unfocused
Mountain and bay, is clean
Forgot, and gone the lumpish sag
Of cloud epitomizing
Our ennui. Storms have blown the sky to blue.

He stops, but less to admire the view
Than to catch breath maybe. Pure gold,
Emerald, violet, ultramarine are blazing
From earth and sea: out there
Croagh Patrick stands uncapped for him.
The old man, shuffling by,
Recalls a rod lost, a dead girl's caress.

Can youthful ecstasies renew
Themselves in blood that has blown so cold?
Nature's more merciful: gently unloosing
His hold upon each care
And human tie, her fingers dim
All lights which held his eye,
And ease him on the last lap to nothingness.

Sailing from Cleggan

Never will I forget it —
Beating out through Cleggan Bay
Towards Inishbofin, how
The shadow lay between us,
An invisible shadow
All but severing us lay
Athwart the Galway hooker.

Sea-room won, turning to port
Round Rossadillisk Point I
Slacken the sheet. Atlantic
Breeze abeam, ahead sun's eye
Opening, we skirt past reefs
And islands — Friar, Cruagh,
Orney, Eeshal, Inishturk.

Porpoises cartwheeling through
Inshore water, boom creaking,
Spray asperging; and sunlight
Transforming to a lime-green
Laughter the lipcurling of
Each morose wave as they burst
On reefs fanged for a shipwreck.

Miracle sun, dispelling
That worst shadow! Salt and sun,
Our wounds' cautery! And how,
Havened, healed, oh lightened of
The shadow, we stepped ashore
On to our recaptured love —
Never could I forget it.

Goldsmith outside Trinity

There he stands, my ancestor, back turned
On Trinity, with his friend Edmund Burke
And others of the Anglo-Irish genius —
Poet, naturalist, historian, hack.

The statue glosses over his uncouth figure,
The pock-marked face, the clownish tongue and mien:
It can say nothing of his unstaunchable charity,
But does full justice to the lack of chin.

Little esteemed by the grave and grey-faced college,
He fiddled his way through Europe, was enrolled
Among the London literates: a deserted
Village brought forth a citizen of the world.

His period and the Anglo-Irish reticence
Kept sentiment unsicklied and unfurred:
Good sense, plain style, a moralist could distinguish
Fine shades from the ignoble to the absurd.

Dublin they flew, the wild geese of Irish culture.
They fly it still: the curdled elegance,
The dirt, the cod, new hucksters, old heroics,
Look better viewed from a remoter stance.

Here from his shadow I note the buses grumbling
On to Rathmines, Stillorgan, Terenure —
Names he'd have known — and think of the arterial
Through-way between us. I would like to be sure

Long-distance genes do more than merely connect us.
But I, a provincial too, an expatriate son
Of Ireland, have nothing of that compulsive gambler,
Nothing of the inspired simpleton.

Yet, as if to an heirloom given a child and long
Unvalued, I at last have returned to him
With gratefuller recognition, get from his shadow
A wordless welcome, a sense of being brought home.

The Whispering Roots

Roots are for holding on, and holding dear.
Mine, like a child's milk teeth, came gently away
From Ireland at the close of my second year.
Is it second childhood now — that I overhear
Them whisper across a lifetime as if from yesterday?

We have had blood enough and talk of blood,
These sixty years. Exiles are two a penny
And race a rancid word; a meaningless word
For the Anglo-Irish: a flighty cuckoo brood
Foisted on alien nests, they knew much pride and many

Falls. But still my roots go whispering on
Like rain on a soft day. Whatever lies
Beneath their cadence I could not disown:
An Irish stranger's voice, its tang and tone,
Recalls a family language I thrill to recognize.

All the melodious places only seen
On a schoolboy's map — Kinsale, Meath, Connemara:
Writers — Swift, Berkeley, Goldsmith, Sheridan:
Fighters, from Vinegar Hill to Stephen's Green:
The Sidhe, saints, scholars, rakes of Mallow, kings of Tara:—

Were background music to my ignorant youth.
Now on a rising wind louder it swells
From the lonely hills of Laois. What can a birth-
Place mean, its features comely or uncouth,
To a long-rootless man? Yet still the place compels.

We Anglo-Irish and the memory of us
Are thinning out. Bad landlords some, some good,
But never a land rightfully ours,
We hunted, fished, swore by our ancestors,
Till we were ripped like parasite growth from native wood.

And still the land compels me; not ancestral
Ghosts, nor regret for childhood's fabled charms,
But a rare peacefulness, consoling, festal,
As if the old religion we oppressed all
Those years folded the stray within a father's arms.

The modern age has passed this island by
And it's the peace of death her revenants find?
Harsh Dublin wit, peasant vivacity
Are here to give your shallow claims the lie.
Perhaps in such soil only the heart's long roots will bind —

Even, transplanted, quiveringly respond
To their first parent earth. Here God is taken
For granted, time like a well-tutored hound
Brought to man's heel, and ghosting underground
Something flows to the exile from what has been forsaken.

In age, body swept on, mind crawls upstream
Toward the source; not thinking to find there
Visions or fairy gold — what old men dream
Is pure restatement of the original theme,
A sense of rootedness, a source held near and dear

Some Beautiful Morning

*'One can't tell whether there won't be a tide to
catch, some beautiful morning.'*
T.H. WHITE

Yes, for the young these expectations charm
There are sealed sailing-orders; but they dream
A cabined breath into the favouring breeze
Kisses a moveless hull alive, will bear
It on to some landfall, no matter where —
The Golden Gate or the Hesperides.

Anchored, they feel the ground-swell of an ocean
Stirring their topmasts with the old illusion
That a horizon can be reached. In pride
Unregimentable as a cross-sea
Lightly they float on pure expectancy.
Some morning now we sail upon the tide.

Wharves, cranes, the lighthouse in a sleep-haze glide
Past them, the landmark spires of home recede,
Glittering waves look like a diadem.
The winds are willing, and the deep is ours
Who chose the very time to weigh the bowers.
How could they know it was the tide caught them?

* * *

Older, they wake one dawn and are appalled,
Rusting in estuary or safely shoaled,
By the impression made on those deep waters.
What most sustained has left a residue
Of cartons, peelings, all such galley spew,
And great loves shrunk to half-submerged french letters.

Sometimes they doubt if ever they left this harbour.
Squalls, calms, the withering wake, frayed ropes and dapper

Refits have thinned back to a dream, dispersed
Like a Spice Island's breath. Who largely tramped
The oceans, to a rotting hulk they're cramped —
Nothing to show for this long toil but waste.

It will come soon — one more spring tide to lift
Us off; the lighthouse and the spire shall drift
Vaguely astern, while distant hammering dies on
The ear. Fortunate they who now can read
Their sailing orders as a firm *God-speed,*
This voyage reaches you beyond the horizon.

A Skull Picked Clean

Blank walls, dead grates, obliterated pages —
Vacancy filled up the house.
Nothing remains of the outward shows,
The inner rages.

Picture collection, trophies, library —
All that entranced, endorsed, enslaved —
With gimcrack ornaments have achieved
Nonentity.

How can I even know what it held most precious,
Its meaning lost, its love consumed?
Silence now where the cool brain hummed:
Where fire was, ashes.

How neatly those rough-tongued removal men
Have done the job. This useless key
They left us when they had earned their pay —
A skull, picked clean.

Hero and Saint

Sad if no one provoked us any more
    To do the improbable —
Catch a winged horse, muck out a preposterous stable,
    Or even some unsensational chore

Like becoming a saint. Those adversaries knew
    The form, to be sure: small use for one
Who after an hour of effort would throw down
    Cross, shovel or lassoo.

It gave more prestige to each prince of lies
    And his far-fetched ordeal
That an attested hero should just fail
    One little finger's breadth from the prize.

Setting for Heracles and Bellerophon
    Such tasks, they judged it a winning gamble,
Forgetting they lived in a world of myth where all
    Conclusions are foregone.

A saint knows patience alone will see him through
    Ordeals which lure, disfigure, numb:
And this (the heroes proved) can only come
    From a star kept in view.

But he forgoes the confidence, the hallowed
    Air of an antique hero:
He never will see himself but as a zero
    Following a One that gives it value.

Hero imagined himself in the constellations,
    Saint as a numbered grain of wheat.
Nowhere but in aspiring do they meet
    And discipline of patience.

He rose to a trial of wit and sinew, *he*
    To improbable heights of loving.
Both, it seems, might have been good for nothing
    Without a consummate adversary.

Sunday Afternoon

'It was like being a child again, listening and thinking
of something else and hearing the voices — endless,
inevitable and restful, like Sunday afternoon.'
Jean Rhys

An inch beyond my groping fingertips,
Lurking just round the corner of the eye.
Bouquet from an empty phial. A sensual ellipse
So it eludes — the quicksilver quarry.

I stretch my hands out to the farther shore,
Between, the fog of Lethe: no river — a mere thread
Bars me from the self I would re-explore:
Powerless I am to break it as the dead.

Yet a picture forms. Summer it must be. Sunlight
Fixes deck-chairs and grass in its motionless torrents.
The rest are shadows. I am the real: but I could run
To those familiar shades for reassurance.

Light slithers from leaf to leaf. Gossip of aspens.
Cool voices blow about, sprinkling the lawn.
Bells hum like a windrush chime of bees: a tolling hastens
Long-skirted loiterers to evensong.

Flowers nod themselves to sleep at last. I smell
Roses — or is it an Irish nursemaid's florin scent?
Gold afternoon rounds to a breast . . . Ah well,
A picture came, though not the one I meant.

Make what you can of it, to recompense
For the real thing, the whole thing vanished beyond recall.
Gauge from a few chance-found and cherished fragments
The genius of the lost original.

A Privileged Moment

Released from hospital, only half alive still,
Cautiously feeling the way back into himself,
Propped up in bed like a guy, he presently ventured
A glance at the ornaments on his mantelshelf.

White, Wedgwood blue, dark lilac coloured or ruby —
Things, you could say, which had known their place and
        price,
Gleamed out at him with the urgency of angels
Eager for him to see through their disguise.

Slowly he turned his head. By gust-flung snatches
A shower announced itself on the windowpane:
He saw unquestioning, not even astonished,
Handfuls of diamonds sprung from a dazzling chain.

Gently at last the angels settled back now
Into mere ornaments, the unearthly sheen
And spill of diamond into familiar raindrops,
It was enough. He'd seen what he had seen.

Philosophy Lectures

He goes about it and about,
By elegant indirections clears a route
To the inmost truth.
Cutting the ground from underneath
Rogue analogies, dialectic tares,
See how he bares
And shames the indulgent, weed-choked soil,
Shaving his field to the strictly meaningful!
Now breathless we
Await, await the epiphany —
A miracle crop to leap from the bald ground

Not one green shoot, however, is discerned.

Well, watch this reaper-and-binder bumbling round
A shuddered field. Proud sheaves collapse
In narrowing squares. A coarser job, perhaps —
Corn, corn cockle and poppy lie
Corded, inseparable. Now each eye
Fastens on that last strand of corn:
Hares, partridge? — no, surely a unicorn
Or phoenix will be harbouring there,
Ripe for revelation. Harvest forgot, I stare
From the field's verge as the last ears fall.

Not even a rabbit emerges. Nothing at all.

Are the two fields identical,
Only the reapers different? Misdirected
Or out of our minds, we expected
A wrong thing — the impossible
Or merely absurd; creatures of fire and fable
Where bread was the intention,
Harvest where harvest was not meant.
Yet in both fields we saw a right end furthered:
Something was gathered.

After an Encaenia

This afternoon the working sparrows, glum
Of plumage, nondescript, flurried, quarrelsome,
Appear as cardinal, kingfisher, hoopoe, bird
Of paradise. They stalk the sward

With gait somnambulous beside their not
So colourful hens, or heart to gorgeous heart
Absently confer together
In tones that do not change to match their feathers.

Will no one tell me what they chirp? I'd say
Their minds are very far away
From this cloud-cuckoo lawn, impatient to
Resume the drudgery sparrows pursue.

Scavengers are they? Gathering crumbs,
Nibbling at particles and old conundrums,
Pouncing on orts never observed before,
They justify their stay-at-home exploring.

I like these scrap-collectors: and to see
Their hard-earned plumes worn without vanity
Hints that a scholar's search for evidence
Is selfless as the lives of saints.

Truth, knowledge even, seems too grandiose
A word for the flair and flutterings of those
Whose ambition is no more wide
Than to get, once for all, one small thing right.

Tenure

is never for keeps, never truly assured
    (tick on, you geological clocks)
though some things almost have it, or seem to have it.
    For example, rocks
in a shivering sea: the castaway who has clawed himself on
    to one:
    a bull's tenacious horn:
    archaic myths: the heroin habit.
Even the sun or a dead man's skull among the cactus
    does not quite have it.

I turn now to American university practice.
    Tenure there is pronounced 'Shangri-
La': once you have it, however spurious
    your fame, not even the angriest
trustees, except for certified madness or moral turpitude,
    can ever dislodge you. I salute
    all those tenurious
professors. But I would not wish to be
one, though the life may be happy and sometimes not
    inglorious.

    Tenure is not for me.
I want to be able to drop out of my head,
or off my rock and swim to another, ringed with a roundelay
of sirens. I should not care to be a dead
    man's skull, or a myth, or a junkie:
    or the too energetic sun.
Since heaven and earth, we are told, shall pass away
    (hell, sneers the blonde, is off already)
I would live each day as if it were my last and first day.

Epitaph for a Drug-Addict

Mourn this young girl. Weep for society
Which gave her little to esteem but kicks.
Impatient of its code, cant, cruelty,
Indifference, she kicked against all pricks
But the dream-loaded hypodermic's. She
Has now obtained an everlasting fix.

Snowfall on a College Garden

While we slept, these formal gardens
Worked into their disguise. The Warden's
Judas and tulip trees awake
In ermine. Here and there a flake
Of white falls from the painted scene,
Or a dark scowl of evergreen
Glares through the shroud, or a leaf dumps
Its load and the soft burden slumps
Earthward like a fainting girl.
No movement else. The blizzard's whirl
Froze to this cataleptic trance
Where nature sleeps and sleep commands
A transformation. See this bush
Furred and fluffed out like a thrush
Against the cold: snow which could snap
A robust veteran branch, piled up
On the razor edge of a weak spray,
Plumping it out in mimicry
Of white buddleia. Like the Elect
Ghosts of summer resurrect
In snowy robes. Only the twangling
Noise of unseen sparrows wrangling
Tells me that my window-view
Holds the garden I once knew.

Remembering Carrownisky

The train window trapped fugitive impressions
As we passed, grasped for a moment then sucked away —
Woods, hills, white farms changing shape and position,
A river which wandered, as if not sure of the way,

Into and off the pane. A landscape less
Well-groomed than, say, a Florentine painter's one,
But its cross-rhythmed shagginess soothed me through the
     glass
As it ambled past out there in the setting sun.

Then, one Welsh mead turned up with a girl rider —
Light hair, red jersey — cantering her horse.
Momently creatures out of some mythical order
Of being they seemed, to justify and endorse

A distrait mood . . . I recalled you at thirteen
Matched against Irish farmers in a race
On Carrownisky — under the cap your dark mane
Streaming, the red windcheater a far-off blaze;

But most how, before the race began, you rode
Slowly round the circuit of sand to calm
The mare and accustom her to a lawless crowd.
Seeing that, I knew you should come to no harm.

Our nerves too can taste of our children's pure
Confidence and grow calm. My daughter rides back
To me down that railside field — elemental, secure
As an image that time may bury but not unmake.

Recurring Dream

. . . the house being the first problem. Dilapidated,
Or is it only half built? He cannot rightly
See or remember. No question it looks unsightly —
All lath and plaster, pipes, treacherous floors
And baffle walls.
                              Before him an assault course
That felt familiar. He infiltrated
The house, wriggling through pipes, circumventing
Holes in the floor, scaling walls; but always
The course gained height. Such was his expertise
He could have done it on his head or blindfold
(Perhaps he did). At least he never failed
To make, or to forget, the happy ending.

For, as he reached it, that bare top storey
Is the highest floor of a luxury hotel
And problem number two. No lift, no stair-well
Visible, and he knows he must get down
To ground level.
                              He'd sensed, during his lone
Climb, others doing the course. Quite solitary
The new ordeal — no chambermaid, waiter, guest
To show him the way out. Frantic he raced
From end to end of the floor. A deep staircase
Appeared at last, pointing the right direction,
Down which he flew; but has no recollection
Where or indeed whether one egressed.

Going My Way?

1

Now, when there is less time than ever,
Every day less time,
I do have the greatest need for patience.

Not to be rushed by thawing, cracking ice
Into a hasty figure.

Not to require daffodils before spring
But accept each spring as another golden handshake.

Not to be misled by fatuous fires
Into a sanctuary clemmed and de-consecrated.

Never irked that this line has no fancy
Departure lounge for V.I.P.s.

Least of all to lose faith in the experience,
The mortal experiment
To which at birth I was committed.

2

Those three provincials, the dear sisters whom
Abrupt catastrophe and slow dry-rot,
Gutting their hearts of youth, condemn to what
Cheerless routines and seasons yet may come —
Would you not say that they were better dead
Than haunted by their sweet illusion's ghost,
Love ground down to irritable dust,
The ideal city still unvisited?

Not so their curtain speech: 'We must go on,
And we must work. Our sufferings will grow

Peace and joy for coming generations.'
Was it illusion's desperate last throw?
At least those heroines showed that nothing can
Become the mortal heart like trust and patience.

At Lemmons

For Jane, Kingsley, Colin, Sargy with much love

Above my table three magnolia flowers
Utter their silent requiems.
Through the window I see your elms
In labour with the racking storm
Giving it shape in April's shifty airs.

Up there sky boils from a brew of cloud
To blue gleam, sunblast, then darkens again.
No respite is allowed
The watching eye, the natural agony.

Below is the calm a loved house breeds
Where four have come together to dwell
— Two write, one paints, the fourth invents —
Each pursuing a natural bent
But less through nature's formative travail
Than each in his own humour finding the self he needs.

Round me all is amenity, a bloom of
Magnolia uttering its requiems,
A climate of acceptance. Very well
I accept my weakness with my friends'
Good natures sweetening every day my sick room.

Translations and Vers d'occasion

The Georgics of Virgil
From Book Two

To begin. Nature is catholic in the propagation of trees.
Some without human help
Spring of their own sweet will and spread abroad by
    winding
Streams and on plains — soft osier, the bending Spanish
    broom,
Poplars, and the pale willow that shows a silver-blue leaf:
Again, some grow from seed they have dropped — the high-
    tiered chestnut,
The common oak, most prolific of leaf among woodland
    trees,
And the oak that in Greece they fancy is able to tell their
    fortune.
Others, like elm and cherry, have a thick undergrowth
Cropping up from their roots: the Parnassian bay-tree also,
When tiny, shelters beneath the immense shade of its
    mother.
Nature gave from the start such modes to evolve the green of
Each tribe of trees in forest, shrubbery, sacred wood.
Others we've found by experience.
One man takes suckers off the tender stock of the mother
And plants them in trenches: another fixes sets in the field
By notching stakes cross-wise or sharpening the wood to a
    point.
Some forest trees there are prefer the pinned-down arches
Of the layer, that make a nursery alive in the parent's earth.
Some need no root, and the pruner
Can safely commit to the soil cuttings from off a high branch.
What's more — and this is a marvel — if you take a saw to
    the trunk of
An olive, a root will come pushing out from the dry wood.

Often again we observe the boughs of one tree change
Without harm into another's — grafted apples growing
On a pear, and stony cherries reddening upon a plum tree.

*   *   *

Oh, spring is good for leaves in the spinney, good to forests,
In spring the swelling earth aches for the seed of new life.
Then the omnipotent Father of air in fruitful showers
Comes down to his happy consort
And greatly breeds upon her great body manifold fruit.
Then are the trackless copses alive with the trilling of birds,
And the beasts look for love, their hour come round again:
Lovely the earth in labour, under a tremulous west wind
The fields unbosom, a mild moisture is everywhere.
Confident grows the grass, for the young sun will not harm it;
The shoots of the vine are not scared of a southerly gale
        arising
Or the sleety rain that slants from heaven beneath a north
        wind, —
No, bravely now they bud and all their leaves display.
So it was, I believe, when the world first began,
Such the illustrious dawning and tenor of their days.
It was springtime then, great spring
Enhanced the earth and spared it the bitter breath of an east
        wind —
A time when the first cattle lapped up the light, and men
Children of earth themselves arose from the raw champaign,
And wild things issued forth in the wood, and stars in the
        sky.
How could so delicate creatures endure the toil they must,
Unless between cold and heat there came this temperate
        spell
And heaven held the earth in his arms and comforted her?

*   *   *

But fortunate too the man who is friends with the country
    gods —
Pan and old Silvanus and the sisterhood of nymphs:
The fasces have no power to disturb him, nor the purple
Of monarchs, nor civil war that sets brother at brother's
    throat,
Nor yet the scheming Dacian as he marches down from the
    Danube,
Nor the Roman Empire itself and kingdoms falling to ruin.
He has no poor to pity, no envy for the rich.
The fruit on the bough, the crops that the field is glad to
    bear
Are his for the gathering: he spares not a glance for the iron
Rigour of law, the municipal racket, the public records.
Other men dare the sea with their oars blindly, or dash
On the sword, or insinuate themselves into royal courts:
One ruins a whole town and the tenements of the poor
In his lust for jewelled cups, for scarlet linen to sleep on;
One piles up great wealth, gloats over his cache of gold;
One gawps at the public speakers; one is worked up to
    hysteria
By the plaudits of senate and people resounding across the
    benches:
These shed their brothers' blood
Merrily, they barter for exile their homes beloved
And leave for countries lying under an alien sun.

From Book Four

Next I come to the manna, the heavenly gift of honey.
Look kindly on this part too, my friend. I'll tell of a tiny
Republic that makes a show well worth your admiration —
Great-hearted leaders, a whole nation whose work is planned,
Their morals, groups, defences — I'll tell you in due order.
A featherweight theme: but one that can load me with fame,
    if only

No wicked fairy cross me, and the Song-god come to my call.
   For a start you must find your bees a suitable home, a
      position
Sheltered from wind (for wind will stop them carrying home
Their forage), a close where sheep nor goats come butting in
To jump on the flowers, nor blundering heifer stray to flick
The dew from the meadow and stamp its springing grasses
      down.
Discourage the lizard, too, with his lapis-lazuli back,
From their rich folds, the bee-eater and other birds,
And the swallow whose breast was blooded once by a
      killer's hand:
For these wreak wholesale havoc, snap up your bees on the
      wing
And bear them off as a tit-bit for their ungentle nestlings.
But mind there's a bubbling spring nearby, a pool moss-
      bordered,
And a rill ghosting through the grass:
See, too, that a palm or tall oleaster shadow the entrance,
For thus, when the new queens lead out the earliest swarms —
The spring all theirs — and the young bees play, from hive
      unprisoned,
The bank may be handy to welcome them in out of the heat
And the tree meet them halfway and make them at home in
      its foliage.
Whether the water flows or is stagnant, fling in the middle
Willow boughs criss-cross and big stones,
That the bees may have plenty of bridges to stand on and
      dry their wings
At the summer sun, in case a shower has caught them
      loitering
Or a gust of east wind ducked them suddenly in the water.
Green spurge-laurel should grow round about, wild thyme
      that perfumes
The air, masses of savory rich-breathing, and violet beds
Sucking the channelled stream.
   Now for the hive itself. Remember, whether you make it
By stitching concave bark or weaving tough withies together

To give it a narrow doorway: for winter grips and freezes
The honey, and summer's melting heat runs it off to waste.
Either extreme is feared by the bees. It is not for fun
That they're so keen on caulking with wax the draughty
        chinks
In their roof, and stuff the rim of their hive with flowery
        pollen,
Storing up for this very job a glue they have gathered
Stickier than bird-lime or pitch from Anatolia.
Often too, if reports are true, they dig deep shelters
Underground and keep house there, or out of the way are
        found
In a sandstone hollow or the heart of a rotten tree.
None the less, you should smear with smooth mud their
        chinky chambers
Solicitously for warmth, and lay a thin dressing of leaves.
Don't have a yew too close to their house, or burn in a
        brazier
Reddening crab-shells: never risk them near a bog,
Or where there's a stink of mud, or a rock formation
        echoes
Hollow when struck and returns your voice like a ghostly
        reflection.
    For the rest, when the golden sun has driven winter to
        ground
And opened up all the leagues of the sky in summer light,
Over the glades and woodlands at once they love to wander
And suck the shining flowers and delicate sip the streams.
Sweet then is their strange delight
As they cherish their children, their nestlings: then with
        craftsmanship they
Hammer out the fresh wax and mould the tacky honey.
Then, as you watch the swarm bursting from hive and
        heavenward
Soaring, and floating there on the limpid air of summer —
A vague and wind-warped column of cloud to your
        wondering eyes: —
Notice them, how they always make for fresh water and leafy

Shelter. Here you shall sprinkle fragrances to their taste —
Crushed balm, honeywort humble —
Make a tinkling noise round about and clash the Mother-god's
    cymbals.
They will settle down of their own accord in the place you
    have perfumed,
And crawl to the innermost room for rest, as their custom is.

The Aeneid of Virgil

From Book Six

Thus he was making petition, his hands upon the altar,
When the Sibyl began to speak:—

                     O child of a goddess' womb,
Trojan son of Anchises, the way to Avernus is easy;
Night and day lie open the gates of death's dark kingdom:
But to retrace your steps, to find the way back to daylight —
That is the task, the hard thing. A few, because of Jove's
Just love, or exalted to heaven by their own flame of
       goodness,
Men born from gods, have done it. Between, there lies a
       forest,
And darkly winds the river Cocytus round the place.
But if so great your love is, so great your passion to cross
The Stygian waters twice and twice behold black Tartarus,
If your heart is set on this fantastic project,
Here's what you must do first. Concealed in a tree's thick
       shade
There is a golden bough — gold the leaves and the tough stem —
Held sacred to Proserpine: the whole wood hides this bough
And a dell walls it round as it were in a vault of shadow.
Yet none is allowed to enter the land which earth conceals
Save and until he has plucked that gold-foil bough from the
       tree.

*   *   *

Aeneas himself, in the middle of these activities,
Carrying the same tools as they, encouraged his friends.
But also, sad at heart, gazing up at the huge forest,
He brooded; and then he uttered his thoughts aloud in a
       prayer:—

If only I might glimpse that golden bough on its tree
In the great wood this very moment! for all that the Sibyl
Said about you, Misenus, was true, too sadly true.
 The words were hardly out when it befell that two doves
Came planing down from above before his very eyes
And alighted upon the green turf. The hero recognised
His mother's birds. His heart leapt up and he said a prayer:—
 Show me the way, if way there is! Oh, wing your flight
To that part of the forest where the precious bough over-
   shadows
The fruitful soil. Do not forsake me, heavenly mother,
At this most crucial hour!
                              He spoke; froze in his tracks
To note what signs they gave and in what direction they'd
   move.
Now the doves, as they fed, flitted on from spot to spot,
   but never
So far ahead that one who followed lost sight of them.
Then, when they came to the mouth of foul-breathing
   Avernus,
Swiftly they soared, went gliding through the soft air and
   settled,
The pair of them, on a tree, the wished-for place, a tree
Amid whose branches there gleamed a bright haze, a
   different colour —
Gold. Just as in depth of winter the mistletoe blooms
In the woods with its strange leafage, a parasite on the tree,
Hanging its yellow-green berries about the smooth round
   boles:
So looked the bough of gold leaves upon that ilex dark,
And in a gentle breeze the gold-foil foliage rustled.
Aeneas at once took hold of the bough, and eagerly breaking
It off with one pull, he bore it into the shrine of the Sibyl.

                    *   *   *

 This done, Aeneas hastened to follow the Sibyl's
   directions.

A deep, deep cave there was, its mouth enormously gaping,
Shingly, protected by the dark lake and the forest gloom:
Above it, no winged creatures could ever wing their way
With impunity, so lethal was the miasma which
Went fuming up from its black throat to the vault of heaven:
Wherefore the Greeks called it Avernus, the Birdless Place.
Here the Sibyl first lined up four black-skinned bullocks,
Poured a libation of wine upon their foreheads, and then,
Plucking the topmost hairs from between their brows, she
        placed
These on the altar fires as an initial offering,
Calling aloud upon Hecate, powerful in heaven and hell.
While others laid their knives to these victims' throats,
        and caught
The fresh warm blood in bowls, Aeneas sacrificed
A black-fleeced lamb to Night, the mother of the Furies,
And her great sister, Earth, and a barren heifer to Proserpine.
Then he set up altars by night to the god of the Underworld,
Laying upon the flames whole carcases of bulls
And pouring out rich oil over the burning entrails.
But listen! — at the very first crack of dawn, the ground
Underfoot began to mutter, the woody ridges to quake,
And a baying of hounds was heard through the half-light:
        the goddess was coming,
Hecate. The Sibyl cried:—
                         Away! Now stand away,
You uninitiated ones, and clear the whole grove!
But you, Aeneas, draw your sword from the scabbard and
        fare forth!
Now you need all your courage, your steadfastness of heart.
    So much she said and, ecstatic, plunged into the opened
        cave mouth:
Unshrinking went Aeneas step for step with his guide.
    You gods who rule the kingdom of souls! You soundless
        shades!
Chaos, and Phlegethon! O mute wide leagues of Nightland! —
Grant me to tell what I have heard! With your assent
May I reveal what lies deep in the gloom of the Underworld!

Dimly through the shadows and dark solitudes they
    wended,
Through the void domiciles of Dis, the bodiless regions:
Just as, through fitful moonbeams, under the moon's thin
    light,
A path lies in a forest, when Jove has palled the sky
With gloom, and the night's blackness has bled the world of
    colour.
See! At the very porch and entrance way to Orcus
Grief and ever-haunting Anxiety make their bed:
Here dwell pallid Diseases, here morose Old Age,
With Fear, ill-prompting Hunger, and squalid Indigence,
Shapes horrible to look at, Death and Agony;
Sleep, too, which is the cousin of Death; and Guilty Joys,
And there, against the threshold, War, the bringer of Death:
Here are the iron cells of the Furies, and lunatic Strife
Whose viperine hair is caught up with a headband soaked in
    blood.
  In the open a huge dark elm tree spreads wide its
    immemorial
Branches like arms, whereon, according to old wives' tales,
Roost the unsolid Dreams, clinging everywhere under its
    foliage.
Besides, many varieties of monsters can be found
Stabled here at the doors—Centaurs and freakish Scyllas,
Briareus with his hundred hands, the Lernaean Hydra
That hisses terribly and the flame-throwing Chimaera,
Gorgons and Harpies, and the ghost of three-bodied Geryon.
Now did Aeneas shake with a spasm of fear, and drawing
His sword, offered its edge against the creatures' onset:
Had not his learned guide assured him they were but
    incorporeal
Existences floating there, forms with no substance behind
    them,
He'd have attacked them, and wildly winnowed with steel
    mere shadows.
  From here is the road that leads to the dismal waters of
    Acheron.

Here a whirlpool boils with mud and immense swirlings
Of water, spouting up all the slimy sand of Cocytus.
A dreadful ferryman looks after the river crossing,
Charon: appallingly filthy he is, with a bush of unkempt
White beard upon his chin, with eyes like jets of fire;
And a dirty cloak draggles down, knotted about his
    shoulders.
He poles the boat, he looks after the sails, he is all the crew
Of that rust-coloured wherry which takes the dead across—
An ancient now, but a god's old age is green and sappy.
This way came fast and streaming up to the bank the whole
    throng:
Matrons and men were there, and there were great-heart
    heroes
Finished with earthly life, boys and unmarried maidens,
Young men laid on the pyre before their parents' eyes;
Multitudinous as the leaves that fall in a forest
At the first frost of autumn, or the birds that out of the
    deep sea
Fly to land in migrant flocks, when the cold of the year
Has sent them overseas in search of a warmer climate.
So they all stood, each begging to be ferried across first,
Their hands stretched out in longing for the shore beyond
    the river.
But the surly ferryman embarks now this, now that group,
While others he keeps away at a distance from the shingle.
Aeneas, being astonished and moved by the great stir, said:—
    Tell me, O Sibyl, what means this rendezvous at the
    river?
What purpose have these souls? By what distinction are
    some
Turned back, while other souls sweep over the wan water?
    To which the long-lived Sibyl uttered this brief reply:—
    O son of Anchises' loins and true-born offspring of
    heaven,
What you see is the mere of Cocytus, the Stygian marsh
By whose mystery even the gods, having sworn, are afraid to
    be forsworn.

312

All this crowd you see are the helpless ones, the unburied:
That ferryman is Charon: the ones he conveys have had
    burial.
None may be taken across from bank to awesome bank of
That harsh-voiced river until his bones are laid to rest.
Otherwise, he must haunt this place for a hundred years
Before he's allowed to revisit the longed-for stream at last.

   The son of Anchises paused and stood stock still, in deep
Meditation, pierced to the heart by pity for their hard
    fortune.
He saw there, sorrowing because deprived of death's fulfil-
    ment,
Leucaspis and Orontes, the commodore of the Lycian
Squadron, who had gone down, their ship being lost with all
    hands
In a squall, sailing with him the stormy seas from Troy.

   And look! yonder was roaming the helmsman, Palinurus,
Who, on their recent voyage, while watching the stars, had
    fallen
From the afterdeck, thrown off the ship there in mid-
    passage.
A sombre form in the deep shadows, Aeneas barely
Recognised him; then accosted:—

                 Which of the gods, Palinurus,
Snatched you away from us and made you drown in the
    mid-sea?
Oh, tell me! For Apollo, whom never before had I found
Untruthful, did delude my mind with this one answer,
Foretelling that you would make your passage to Italy
Unharmed by sea. Is it thus he fufils a sacred promise?

   Palinurus replied:—

             The oracle of Phoebus has not tricked you,
My captain, son of Anchises; nor was I drowned by a god.
It was an accident: I slipped, and the violent shock
Of my fall broke off the tiller to which I was holding firmly
As helmsman, and steering the ship. By the wild seas I swear
That not on my own account was I frightened nearly so
    much as

Lest your ship, thus crippled, its helmsman overboard,
Lose steerage-way and founder amid the mountainous waves.
Three stormy nights did the South wind furiously drive me
    along
Over the limitless waters: on the fourth day I just
Caught sight of Italy, being lifted high on a wave crest.
Little by little I swam to the shore. I was all but safe,
When, as I clung to the rough-edged cliff top, my fingers
    crooked
And my soaking garments weighing me down, some
    barbarous natives
Attacked me with swords, in their ignorance thinking that I
    was a rich prize.
Now the waves have me, the winds keep tossing me up on
    the shore again.
So now, by the sweet light and breath of heaven above
I implore you, and by your father, by your hopes of grow-
    ing Ascanius
Redeem me from this doom, unconquered one! Please
    sprinkle
Dust on my corpse — you can do it and quickly get back to
    port Velia:
Or else, if way there is, some way that your heavenly mother
Is showing you (not, for sure, without the assent of deity
Would you be going to cross the swampy Stygian stream),
Give poor Palinurus your hand, take me with you across the
    water
So that at least I may rest in the quiet place, in death.
    Thus did the phantom speak, and the Sibyl began to
    speak thus:—
    This longing of yours, Palinurus, has carried you quite
    away.
Shall you, unburied, view the Styx, the austere river
Of the Infernal gods, or come to its bank unbidden?
Give up this hope that the course of fate can be swerved
    by prayer.
But hear and remember my words, to console you in your
    hard fortune.

314

I say that the neighbouring peoples, compelled by portents
    from heaven
Occurring in every township, shall expiate your death,
Shall give you burial and offer the solemn dues to your
    grave,
And the place shall keep the name of Palinurus for ever.

*   *   *

Thus spoke the long-lived priestess of Phoebus, then
    added this:—
But come, resume your journey, finish the task in hand!
Let us go quickly on. I can see the bastions, forged in
The Cyclops' furnaces, and the arch of the gateway yonder,
Where we are bidden to put down your passport, the golden
    bough.
    She had spoken. Side by side they went the twilight way,
Rapidly covering the space between, and approached the
    gateway.
Aeneas stopped at the entrance, sprinkled himself with holy
Water, and placed the bough right at the doorway there.
    Now this was done at last, and Proserpine had her
    offering,
They went on into the Happy Place, the green and genial
Glades where the fortunate live, the home of the blessed
    spirits.
What largesse of bright air, clothing the vales in dazzling
Light, is here! This land has a sun and stars of its own.
Some exercise upon the grassy playing-fields
Or wrestle on the yellow sands in rivalry of sport;
Some foot the rhythmic dances and chant poems aloud.
Orpheus, the Thracian bard, is there in his long robe,
To accompany their measures upon the seven-stringed lyre
Which he plucks, now with his fingers, now with an ivory
    plectrum.
Here is the ancient line of Teucer, a breed most handsome,
Great-hearted heroes born in the happier days of old,
Ilus, Assaracus, and Dardanus, founder of Troy.

315

From afar Aeneas marvelled at the arms, the phantom
    chariots.
Spears stood fixed in the ground, everywhere over the plain
Grazed the unharnessed horses. The pleasure those heroes
    had felt,
When alive, in their arms and chariots, the care they had
    taken to pasture
Their sleek horses — all was the same beyond the tomb.

*   *   *

Now bend your gaze this way, look at that people there!
They are *your* Romans. Caesar is there and all Ascanius'
Posterity, who shall pass beneath the arch of day.
And here, here is the man, the promised one you know of —
Caesar Augustus, son of a god, destined to rule
Where Saturn ruled of old in Latium, and there
Bring back the age of gold: his empire shall expand
Past Garamants and Indians to a land beyond the zodiac
And the sun's yearly path, where Atlas the sky-bearer pivots
The wheeling heavens, embossed with fiery stars, on his
    shoulder.
Even now the Caspian realm, the Crimean country
Tremble at oracles of the gods predicting his advent,
And the seven mouths of the Nile are in a lather of fright.
Not even Hercules roved so far and wide over earth,
Although he shot the bronze-footed deer, brought peace to
    the woods of
Erymanthus, subdued Lerna with the terror of his bow;
Nor Bacchus, triumphantly driving his team with vines for
    reins,
His team of tigers down from Mount Nysa, travelled so far.
Do we still hesitate, then, to enlarge our courage by action?
Shrink from occupying the territory of Ausonia?

*   *   *

So far and wide, surveying all,
They wandered through that region, those broad and hazy
    plains.
After Anchises had shown his son over the whole place
And fired his heart with passion for the great things to come,
He told the hero of wars he would have to fight one day,
Told of the Laurentines and the city of Latinus,
And how to evade, or endure, each crisis upon his way.
    There are two gates of Sleep: the one is made of horn,
They say, and affords the outlet for genuine apparitions:
The other's a gate of brightly-shining ivory; this way
The Shades send up to earth false dreams that impose upon
    us.
Talking, then, of such matters, Anchises escorted his son
And the Sibyl as far as the ivory gate and sent them through
    it.
Aeneas made his way back to the ships and his friends with
    all speed,
Then coasted along direct to the harbour of Caieta.
The ships, anchored by the bows, line the shore with their
    sterns.

The Eclogues of Virgil

Eclogue 4

Sicilian Muse, I would try now a somewhat grander theme.
Shrubberies or meek tamarisks are not for all: but if it's
Forests I sing, may the forests be worthy of a consul.
    Our is the crowning era foretold in prophecy:
Born of Time, a great new cycle of centuries
Begins. Justice returns to earth, the Golden Age
Returns, and its first-born comes down from heaven above.

317

Look kindly, chaste Lucina, upon this infant's birth,
For with him shall hearts of iron cease, and hearts of gold
Inherit the whole earth — yes, Apollo reigns now.
And it's while you are consul — you, Pollio — that this
        glorious
Age shall dawn, the march of its great months begin.
You at our head, mankind shall be freed from its age-long
        fear,
All stains of our past wickedness being cleansed away.
This child shall enter into the life of the gods, behold them
Walking with antique heroes, and himself be seen of them,
And rule a world made peaceful by his father's virtuous acts.
    Child, your first birthday presents will come from
        nature's wild —
Small presents: earth will shower you with romping ivy,
        foxgloves,
Bouquets of gipsy lilies and sweetly-smiling acanthus.
Goats shall walk home, their udders taut with milk, and
        nobody
Herding them: the ox will have no fear of the lion:
Silk-soft blossom will grow from your very cradle to lap you.
But snakes will die, and so will fair-seeming, poisonous plants.
Everywhere the commons will breathe of spice and incense.
    But when you are old enough to read about famous men
And your father's deeds, to comprehend what manhood
        means,
Then a slow flush of tender gold shall mantle the great plains,
Then shall grapes hang wild and reddening on thorn-trees,
And honey sweat like dew from the hard bark of oaks.
Yet there'll be lingering traces still of our primal error,
Prompting us to dare the seas in ships, to girdle
Our cities round with walls and break the soil with plough-
        shares.
A second Argo will carry her crew of chosen heroes,
A second Tiphys steer her. And wars — yes, even wars
There'll be; and great Achilles must sail for Troy again.
    Later, when the years have confirmed you in full man-
        hood,

318

Traders will retire from the sea, from the pine-built vessels
They used for commerce: every land will be self-supporting.
The soil will need no harrowing, the vine no pruning-knife;
And the tough ploughman may at last unyoke his oxen.
We shall stop treating wool with artificial dyes,
For the ram himself in his pasture will change his fleece's
    colour,
Now to a charming purple, now to a saffron hue,
And grazing lambs will dress themselves in coats of scarlet.
    'Run, looms, and weave this future!' — thus have the
        Fates spoken,
In unison with the unshakeable intent of Destiny.
    Come soon, dear child of the gods, Jupiter's great viceroy!
Come soon — the time is near — to begin your life illustrious!
Look how the round and ponderous globe bows to salute
        you,
The lands, the stretching leagues of sea, the unplumbed sky!
Look how the whole creation exults in the age to come!
    If but the closing days of a long life were prolonged
For me, and I with breath enough to tell your story,
Oh then I should not be worsted at singing by Thracian
        Orpheus
Or Linus — even though Linus were backed by Calliope
His mother, and Orpheus by his father, beauteous Apollo.
Should Pan compete with me, and Arcady judge us, even
Pan, great Pan, with Arcadian judges, would lose the contest.
    Begin, dear babe, and smile at your mother to show you
        know her —
This is the tenth month now, and she is sick of waiting.
Begin, dear babe. The boy who does not smile at his mother
Will never deserve to sup with a god or sleep with a goddess.

Eclogue 10

One task, my last, I pray you to favour me in, Arethusa —
A little poem for Gallus, my friend: no one could grudge him

A poem; and may it be read by Lycoris too, his love.
Arethusa, when you stream beneath the Sicilian waters,
I wish your purity be not sullied with bitter brine:
And so I begin. While snub-nosed she-goats browse upon
Soft shoots, I'll tell of Gallus and the anguish of his heart.
Not to deaf ears I sing, for the woods echo my singing.
    Young Naiads, oh where were you, haunting what wood-
        land glades
Or groves, that time my Gallus was sick with hopeless love?
No duties kept you upon the ridges of Mount Parnassus
Or Pindus, or by the sacred spring at Helicon's foot.
Even the laurels, even the tamarisks wept for him
Where under a crag he lay, alone: even pine-clad Maenalus
Wept in pity for him, and the cold cliffs of Lycaeus.
    The sheep were standing round you — they see no shame
        in our sorrows,
So think no shame of them, my heaven-sent poet: even
Exquisite Adonis grazed sheep beside a stream.
The shepherd was there, and the swineherds heavy of gait,
        and Menalcas —
Wet he was from soaking acorns for winter mash.
'What fired this passion of yours?' they asked: and Apollo
        came
And said, 'You have lost your senses, Gallus. Your loved
        Lycoris
Has gone with another man, through snows and rough
        encampments.'
Silvanus also came, in rustic coronet — flowers of
Fennel and long-stemmed lilies tossing upon his head.
Pan came, the god of Arcady, guised as I've often seen him,
Vermilion-stained with the juice of elderberries: he said,
'Weep you no more. The Love-god has no compassion for
        sorrow.
Goats never have enough of leafage, nor bees of clover,
Nor grass of runnels; and weeping can never appease the
        Love-god.'
    But Gallus, sick at heart, said, 'Arcadians, you'll be
    singing

The tale of my love to your mountains, whatever befall.
    You are masters
Of music, you Arcadians. How tranquil my bones would
    rest,
If over them your reed-pipes were making my love immortal!
Ah but I wish I had been of your company, and lived here
A shepherd of your sheep or a worker in these vineyards.
Why, then I should have had a Phyllis, an Amyntas —
Some flame or other — to lie with among the sally trees
Sheltered by drooping vines. Amyntas is dark? But look at
Violets or blueberries — they have the same dusky glow.
Phyllis would pick me garlands, Amyntas sing for me.
    'Soft meads, cool streams you would find here, and
        woodlands, dear Lycoris —
A paradise where we could have grown old together.
But I'm a soldier, forced by insensate zeal for the War-god
To go where weapons fly and the foe's in battle formation.
And you — how hard it is to believe you have left your
        country:
Far off among Alpine snows or over the frozen Rhine
You pass, and I'm not there. Oh may the cold not hurt you!
May splintering ice not gash your delicate feet, Lycoris!
    'But I shall go and set to music for the Sicilian
Shepherd's pipe the poems I wrote in Chalcidic verse.
I shall live hard in the forest, where wild beasts have their
        lairs —
My mind is made up — and cut the name of my loved
        Lycoris
Upon the young trees' bark: my love will grow as the trees
        grow.
I'll roam the slopes of Maenalus with bevies of nymphs the
        while,
Or hunt the vicious boar: however cold it is,
I'll whistle my hounds to cast about the Parthenian coverts.
I picture myself already, scaling the crags, hallooing
Through the wide woods, letting fly with Cretan arrows
        there
To my heart's content.

'As if such things could drug a frenzy like mine!
As if men's agonies could soften the Love-god's nature!
No, never again shall I find solace among the wood-nymphs,
Or in poetry even: words and woods mean nothing to me
      now.
No ordeal I could suffer would change the Love-god's heart,
Though in the deep midwinter I drank from Thracian
      streams
And offered myself to the sleety blizzards of Macedonia;
Or though I became a nomad shepherd beneath the searing
African sun, which scorches and kills the very elm bark.
All-conquering is Love — no use to fight against him.'
   Muses divine, may you be satisfied with these verses
Your poet has sung while he sat here, weaving a basket of
      slender
Marsh-mallow stems. And I pray you, make them acceptable
To Gallus, for whom my love grows greater all the time
As the green alder-tree grows fast in early spring.
Now must I go. The shade of this juniper turns chill.
Shade stunts a crop, and it's bad for a singer's voice. My goats,
You have pastured well, the twilight deepens — home then,
      home!

The Graveyard by the Sea

(From Paul Valéry)

This quiet roof, where dove-sails saunter by,
Between the pines, the tombs, throbs visibly.
Impartial noon patterns the sea in flame —
That sea for ever starting and re-starting.
When thought has had its hour, oh how rewarding
Are the long vistas of celestial calm!

What grace of light, what pure toil goes to form
The manifold diamond of the elusive foam!
What peace I feel begotten at that source!
When sunlight rests upon a profound sea,
Time's air is sparkling, dream is certainty —
Pure artifice both of an eternal Cause.

Sure treasure, simple shrine to intelligence,
Palpable calm, visible reticence,
Proud-lidded water, Eye wherein there wells
Under a film of fire such depth of sleep —
O silence ! . . . Mansion in my soul, you slope
Of gold, roof of a myriad golden tiles.

Temple of time, within a brief sigh bounded,
To this rare height inured I climb, surrounded
By the horizons of a sea-girt eye.
And, like my supreme offering to the gods,
That peaceful coruscation only breeds
A loftier indifference on the sky.

Even as a fruit's absorbed in the enjoying,
Even as within the mouth its body dying
Changes into delight through dissolution,
So to my melted soul the heavens declare
All bounds transfigured into a boundless air,
And I breathe now my future's emanation.

Beautiful heaven, true heaven, look how I change!
After such arrogance, after so much strange
Idleness — strange, yet full of potency —
I am all open to these shining spaces;
Over the homes of the dead my shadow passes,
Ghosting along — a ghost subduing me.

My soul laid bare to your midsummer fire,
O just, impartial light whom I admire,
Whose arms are merciless, you have I stayed
And give back, pure, to your original place.
Look at yourself . . . But to give light implies
No less a sombre moiety of shade.

Oh, for myself alone, mine, deep within
At the heart's quick, the poem's fount, between
The void and its pure issue, I beseech
The intimations of my secret power.
O bitter, dark and echoing reservoir
Speaking of depths always beyond my reach.

But know you — feigning prisoner of the boughs,
Gulf which eats up their slender prison-bars,
Secret which dazzles though mine eyes are closed —
What body drags me to its lingering end,
What mind draws *it* to this bone-peopled ground?
A star broods there on all that I have lost.

Closed, hallowed, full of insubstantial fire,
Morsel of earth to heaven's light given o'er —
This plot, ruled by its flambeaux, pleases me —
A place all gold, stone and dark wood, where shudders
So much marble above so many shadows:
And on my tombs, asleep, the faithful sea.

Keep off the idolaters, bright watch-dog, while —
A solitary with the shepherd's smile —
I pasture long my sheep, my mysteries,

324

My snow-white flock of undisturbéd graves!
Drive far away from here the careful doves,
The vain daydreams, the angels' questioning eyes!

Now present here, the future takes its time.
The brittle insect scrapes at the dry loam;
All is burnt up, used up, drawn up in air
To some ineffably rarefied solution . . .
Life is enlarged, drunk with annihilation,
And bitterness is sweet, and the spirit clear.

The dead lie easy, hidden in earth where they
Are warmed and have their mysteries burnt away.
Motionless noon, noon aloft in the blue
Broods on itself — a self-sufficient theme.
O rounded dome and perfect diadem,
I am what's changing secretly in you.

I am the only medium for your fears.
My penitence, my doubts, my baulked desires —
These are the flaw within your diamond pride . . .
But in their heavy night, cumbered with marble,
Under the roots of trees a shadow people
Has slowly now come over to your side.

To an impervious nothingness they're thinned,
For the red clay has swallowed the white kind;
Into the flowers that gift of life has passed.
Where are the dead? — their homely turns of speech,
The personal grace, the soul informing each?
Grubs thread their way where tears were once composed.

The bird-sharp cries of girls whom love is teasing,
The eyes, the teeth, the eyelids moistly closing,
The pretty breast that gambles with the flame,
The crimson blood shining when lips are yielded,
The last gift, and the fingers that would shield it —
All go to earth, go back into the game.

And you, great soul, is there yet hope in you
To find some dream without the lying hue
That gold or wave offers to fleshly eyes?
Will you be singing still when you're thin air?
All perishes. A thing of flesh and pore
Am I. Divine impatience also dies.

Lean immortality, all crêpe and gold,
Laurelled consoler frightening to behold,
Death is a womb, a mother's breast, you feign —
The fine illusion, oh the pious trick!
Who does not know them, and is not made sick —
That empty skull, that everlasting grin?

Ancestors deep down there, O derelict heads
Whom such a weight of spaded earth o'erspreads,
Who *are* the earth, in whom our steps are lost,
The real flesh-eater, worm unanswerable
Is not for you that sleep under the table:
Life is his meat, and I am still his host.

'Love', shall we call him? 'Hatred of self', maybe?
His secret tooth is so intimate with me
That any name would suit him well enough,
Enough that he can see, will, daydream, touch —
My flesh delights him, even upon my couch
I live but as a morsel of his life.

Zeno, Zeno, cruel philosopher Zeno,
Have you then pierced me with your feathered arrow
That hums and flies, yet does not fly! The sounding
Shaft gives me life, the arrow kills. Oh, sun! —
Oh, what a tortoise-shadow to outrun
My soul, Achilles' giant stride left standing!

No, no! Arise! The future years unfold.
Shatter, O body, meditation's mould!
And, O my breast, drink in the wind's reviving!

A freshness, exhalation of the sea,
Restores my soul . . . Salt-breathing potency!
Let's run at the waves and be hurled back to living!

Yes, mighty sea with such wild frenzies gifted
(The panther skin and the rent chlamys), sifted
All over with sun-images that glisten,
Creature supreme, drunk on your own blue flesh,
Who in a tumult like the deepest hush
Bite at your sequin-glittering tail — yes, listen!

The wind is rising! . . . We must try to live!
The huge air opens and shuts my book: the wave
Dares to explode out of the rocks in reeking
Spray. Fly away, my sun-bewildered pages!
Break, waves! Break up with your rejoicing surges
This quiet roof where sails like doves were pecking.

The Voyage

(From Baudelaire)

1

Children, in love with maps and gravings, know
A universe the size of all they lack.
How big the world is by their lamps' clear glow!
But ah, how small to memory looking back!

One morning we set out, our heads on fire,
Our yearning hearts sulky with sour unease,
Following the waves' rhythm, nursing our desire
For the unbounded on those earth-bound seas.

Some glad to leave an infamous birthplace: some
To escape the cradle's nightmare; and a few —
Star-gazers drowned in a woman's eyes — it's from
The scent and power of Circe that they flew.

Not to be changed to beasts, they drug their minds
With space and the large light and burning sky:
The ice that bites them and the suns that bronze
Efface the scar of kisses gradually.

But the true travellers are those who go
For going's sake: hearts light as a balloon,
They never slip their fate: why it is so
They cannot tell, but the word is 'Fare on!'

With longings shaped like hazy clouds, they dream —
As a recruit of gunfire — there impend
Huge pleasures, changeful and untried, whose fame
Is past the wit of man to comprehend.

2

God, that we should behave like top and ball
Bouncing and twirling! Even in our sleep
The Unknown we seek gives us no rest at all,
Like suns tormented by an Angel's whip.

Strange game, whose goal is always on the move
And being nowhere, may be any place;
And Man, whose hope no setbacks will disprove,
Keeps running madly just to catch repose.

The soul is a three-master, Ithaca-bound.
'Keep your eyes skinned!' a sea voice will implore;
From the maintop a keen, mad voice resound
'Love . . . glory . . . luck!' Oh hell, we've run ashore!

Each little isle hailed by the look-out man
Is the Promised Land, golden beyond belief:
Such revels he imagines, but he'll scan
By the cold light of dawn only a reef.

Fairytale lands — that they should craze him so!
Clap him in irons? Pitch him overboard? —
This bold Columbus, drunken matelot,
Whose mirage makes our sea more hard to abide.

So the old tramp goes pounding through the shit
And, nose in air, dreams up a paradise;
The meanest shanties where a candle's lit
Are Pleasure-Domes to his enchanted eyes.

3

Amazing voyagers, what splendid tales
Your sea-deep eyes have printed on them. Rare
The jewel caskets of your chronicles:
Show us those gems, fashioned from stars and air.

We'd voyage, but we have no sail or screw.
Liven our spirits, that are canvas-taut.
Breathe your horizon memories, view on view,
Over the boredom of our prisoned thought.

Tell us, what have you seen?

4

                              We've seen some stars,
Some waves; and we have met with sand-banks too:
For all the uncharted hazards and the jars
We suffered, we were often bored, like you.

Splendour of sunlight on a violet sea,
Splendour of townships in the setting sun
Kindled in us a burning wish to be
Deep in a sky whose mirror lured us on.

Rich towns and landscapes lovely to the gaze
Had never the mysterious appeal
Of those that chance created out of haze
And our impassioned wanting made so real.

Enjoying gives desire more potency —
Desire that feeds on pleasure: the bark grows
Thicker and tougher on the ageing tree,
But its boughs strain to see the sun more close.

Will you be growing still, great tree, who soared
Higher than cypress? . . . Well, since you rejoice
To swallow anything far-fetched, we've worked hard
And brought these sketches for your album, boys.

There we have greeted trumpeting effigies,
Thrones of star-clustered gems dazzling to view,
Palaces wrought by fairy artifice —
Dreams that would bankrupt millionaires like you;

Dresses which stagger you like drunkenness,
Women with nails and teeth vermilion-stained,
Magicians conjuring a snake's caress.

5

Yes, yes! Go on! and then?

6

You baby-brained!

Lest we should miss the great, the unique thing,
Ubiquitous and unconcealed we've seen
On the predestined ladder's every rung
The tedious sight of man's inveterate sin:

Woman, bitch slave, stupid and overweening,
Vain without humour, and without disgust
Self-loving; man, slave to a slave, a stream in
A sewer, all grab and foulness, greed, power, lust:

The thug who loves his work, the sobbing martyr,
The feast that seasons and perfumes the blood;
The prince whom power corrupts into self-murder,
The mob who kiss the brutalizing rod:

Several religions, just like our own following,
Bulldoze their path to heaven; the austere,
While dissolute types on feather beds are wallowing,
Gratify their own taste with nails and hair:

Gabbling mankind, drunk on its own nature
And mad today as in all previous years,
Raving with agony bawls to its Maker
'My lord, oh my twin-brother, it's you I curse!'

And the least mad, tough lovers of Alienation,
Fleeing the herd whom fate has corralled in,
Take refuge with a limitless Illusion . . .
Such is our globe's unchanging bulletin.

7

Acid the knowledge travellers draw. The world,
Little and dull, today, tomorrow and
Tomorrow makes you see yourself — an appalled
Oasis in a tedium of sand.

Should we then go, or stay? If you can, stay:
Go, if you must. One races: one shams death
To cheat the watchful enemy of his prey.
Some runners Time allows no pause for breath —

The wandering Jew, the apostles, who can neither
Escape this gladiator and his net
By ship nor car nor any means: another
Can kill Time without stirring from his cot.

And when he sets his foot upon our spine
At last, we shall cry hopefully 'Let's be going!'
Just as in old days when we left for China,
Eyes fixed on distances and our hair blowing,

We shall embark upon the sea of Shade,
Light-hearted as a young enthusiast.
Now do you hear those voices, sweet and sad,
Singing, 'This way, all you who want to taste

The fragrant lotus! Here we shall let you savour
Those miracle fruits, for which your souls were famished:
Come and transport yourselves with the strange flavour
Of a long afternoon that's never finished'?

What's grown unreal, we guess from its usual tone.
Dear friends stretch out their arms; and 'Swim this way,
Take new life from my loyal heart,' cries one
Whose knees we kissed — but that was yesterday.

8

Old Captain Death, it's time to go. We're sick
Of this place. Weigh anchor! Set the course, and steer!
Maybe the sky and sea are inky black,
But in our hearts — you know them — all is clear.

Pour us the cordial that kills and cheers.
We wish, for our whole beings burn and burn,
To sound the abyss — heaven or hell, who cares? —
And find the secret wombed in the Unknown.

Vers d'occasion

Tuscany*

Tuscany, long endeared to English hearts —
Vine, olive, maize, glories of song and stone —
We mourned your dead when chaos broke upon
That ordered life of husbandry and arts.
And we lament your treasures so defaced.
All beauty which the vandal floods have blurred,
All wrecked originals of brush and wood
Are pages torn for ever out of our living past.

The muddied inundations fall away
From cities and man's heart. He'll count the score,

Then put his house to rights and turn once more
To face the mountainous challenges. Nature may
Still overwhelm us: but from nature's hand
Issues the clay we shape to an immortal end.

*This poem was written for Laurence Olivier to read at
a gala performance in aid of the Florentine Flood appeal.

A Short Dirge for
St. Trinian's*

Where are the girls of yesteryear? How strange
To think they're scattered East, South, West and North —
Those pale Medusas of the Upper Fourth,
Those Marihuanas of the Moated Grange.

No more the shrieks of victims, and no more
The fiendish chuckle borne along the breeze!
Gone are the basilisk eyes, the bony knees.
Mice, and not blood, run down each corridor.

Now poison ivy twines the dorm where casks
Were broached and music mistresses were flayed,
While on the sports ground where the pupils played
The relatively harmless adder basks.

Toll for St. Trinian's, nurse of frightful girls!
St. Trinian's, mother of the far too free!
No age to come (thank God) will ever see
Such an academy as Dr. Searle's.

*A poem written on the occasion of Ronald Searle's decision
to kill off St. Trinian's. From 'Souls in Torment' by Ronald
Searle, Perpetua Ltd, 1953.

Cat*

Tearaway kitten or staid mother of fifty,
Persian, Chinchilla, Siamese
Or backstreet brawler — you all have a tiger in your blood
And eyes opaque as the sacred mysteries.

The hunter's instinct sends you pouncing, dallying,
Formal and wild as a temple dance.
You take from men what is your due — the fireside saucer,
And give him his — a purr of tolerance.

Like poets you wrap your solitude around you
And catch your meaning unawares:
With consequential trot or frantic tarantella
You follow up your top-secret affairs.

Simpkin, our pretty cat, assumes my lap
As a princess her rightful throne,
Pads round and drops asleep there. Each is a familiar
Warmth to the other, each no less alone.

A poem commissioned for a book about cats.

Another Day*

Through the hand's skill gradually
The head learnt its identity.
The shaping hand was touched and led
By the poem in the head.
Head and hand each went its own
Way, yet in strange unison.
Certainly the pair had set
Out by different routes; and yet
Their destination was the same.

A demon, jealous of the fame
That crowns the hard creative game,
BLEW — and turned back to brutish clay
The breathing replica of Day.
But Day survived and K. contrived
To keep her head and bring Day's head
To life again another day.

*K. is the sculptress Kathleen Schwarzenberg who in May
1970 modelled Day Lewis's head in clay preparatory to
casting it. That night a storm blew up which smashed
the finished mould to smithereens. Undaunted, the
sculptress started again from scratch, successfully.

Battle of Britain*

What did we earth-bound make of it? A tangle
Of vapour trails, a vertiginously high
Swarming of midges, at most a fiery angel
Hurled out of heaven, was all we could descry.

How could we know the agony and pride
That scrawled those fading signatures up there,
And the cool expertise of them who died
Or lived through that delirium of the air?

*The first two verses of a poem written for the Première of a
film about the Battle of Britain.*

Index of Titles

Index of First Lines

350